Guide to IELTS

The International English Language Testing System (IELTS) is jointly managed by the British Council, Cambridge ESOL Examinations and IDP Education, Australia.

There are two versions of the test:

- Academic
- General Training.

The Academic test is for students wishing to study at undergraduate or postgraduate level in an English-medium environment.

The General Training test is for people who wish to migrate to an English-speaking country.

There are separate Reading and Writing components for the Academic and General Training IELTS tests.

The test
There are four components to the test.

Listening   30 minutes, plus 10 minutes for transferring answers to the answer sheet.
There are 4 sections in this part of the test.

Reading   60 minutes. There are 3 texts in this component, with 40 questions to answer.

Writing   60 minutes. There are 2 writing tasks. Your answer for Task 1 should have a minimum of 150 words. Your answer for Task 2 should have a minimum of 250 words.

Speaking   11–14 minutes. There are 3 parts in this component. This part of the test will be recorded.

Timetabling – Listening, Reading and Writing must be taken on the same day, and in the order listed above. Speaking can be taken up to seven days before or after the other components.

Scoring – Each component of the test is given a band score. The average of the four scores produces the Overall Band Score. You do not pass or fail IELTS; you receive a score.

IELTS and the Common European Framework of Reference
The CEFR shows the level of the learner and is used for many English as a Foreign Language examinations. The table below shows the approximate CEFR level and the equivalent IELTS Overall Band Score.

CEFR description	CEFR code	IELTS Band Score
Proficient user (Advanced)	C2 C1	9 7–8
Independent user (Intermediate – Upper Intermediate)	B2 B1	5–6.5 4–5

This table contains the general descriptors for the band scores 1–9.

IELTS Band Scores		
9	Expert user	Has fully operational command of the language: appropriate, accurate and fluent with complete understanding
8	Very good user	Has fully operational command of the language, with only occasional unsystematic inaccuracies and inappropriacies. Misunderstandings may occur in unfamiliar situations. Handles complex detailed argumentation well

7	Good user	Has operational command of the language, though with occasional inaccuracies, inappropriacies and misunderstandings in some situations. Generally handles complex language well and understands detailed reasoning
6	Competent user	Has generally effective command of the language despite some inaccuracies, inappropriacies and misunderstandings. Can use and understand fairly complex language, particularly in familiar situations
5	Modest user	Has partial command of the language, coping with overall meaning in most situations, though is likely to make many mistakes. Should be able to handle basic communication in own field
4	Limited user	Basic competence is limited to familiar situations. Has frequent problems in understanding and expression. Is not able to use complex language
3	Extremely limited user	Conveys and understands only general meaning in very familiar situations. Frequent breakdowns in communication occur
2	Intermittent user	No real communication is possible except for the most basic information using isolated words or short formulae in familiar situations and to meet immediate needs. Has great difficulty understanding spoken and written English
1	Non user	Essentially has no ability to use the language beyond possibly a few isolated words
0	Did not attempt the test	No assessable information provided

Marking

The Listening and Reading components have 40 items, each worth one mark if correctly answered. Here are some examples of how marks are translated into band scores.

Listening 16 out of 40 correct answers: band score 5
23 out of 40 correct answers: band score 6
30 out of 40 correct answers: band score 7

Reading 15 out of 40 correct answers: band score 5
23 out of 40 correct answers: band score 6
30 out of 40 correct answers: band score 7

Writing and Speaking are marked according to performance descriptors.

Writing – Examiners award a band score for each of four areas with equal weighting:

- Task achievement (Task 1)
- Task response (Task 2)
- Coherence and cohesion
- Lexical resource and grammatical range and accuracy

Speaking – Examiners award a band score for each of four areas with equal weighting:

- Fluency and coherence
- Lexical resource
- Grammatical range
- Accuracy and pronunciation

For full details of how the examination is scored and marked, go to: **www.ielts.org.**

Unit 1

Family

Speaking

Talking about your own life and experience in Speaking Part 1

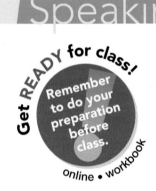

Get READY for class!
Remember to do your preparation before class.
online • workbook

Develop your exam skills

info

The complete Speaking test takes 11–14 minutes. The examiner asks questions and you give answers. The answers are recorded.

Part 1: Introduction and interview

- Part 1 takes 4–5 minutes.
- In the introduction, the examiner introduces himself/herself to you. He/She asks you to confirm your identity.
- Then the interview starts. The examiner asks you questions on general topics, e.g. family, hobbies, studying.
- Part 1 tests your ability to understand general questions and to give relevant answers. It also tests your ability to expand your answers.

 1 **You will hear the examiner's instructions in Part 1. Read the examiner's instructions before you listen and try to complete any gaps you can. Then listen and complete the instructions.**

Hello. My (**1**) .... is Steve Smith. Could you tell me your (**2**) .... , please?

Thank you. Can you show me your (**3**) .... , please?

I'd now like to ask you some questions about yourself.

Tell me about your (**4**) ....

What does your father (**5**) .... ?

(**6**) .... much time do you spend with your family?

Are people in your (**7**) .... close to their family?

Do you prefer to go out with your family or your (**8**) .... ?

Where do you (**9**) .... at the moment?

 2 **Listen to a candidate answering a question from Exercise 1. Which question is it? What do you remember about the student's answer?**

3 **Listen to the candidate's answer again. Rate it out of 5, where 1 is poor and 5 is excellent. Then choose the best description.**

1 The information in the answer is *relevant / not relevant*.

2 The answer is *very short / OK / very long*.

3 The candidate speaks *with pauses / at normal speed / very fast*.

4 The vocabulary is *relevant / not relevant* to the topic.

5 The pronunciation is *poor / OK / clear*.

6 There are *a lot of errors / one or two errors / no errors* in the grammar.

see **GRAMMAR** page 142 and more **PRACTICE** online

4 **Prepare to answer the question yourself. Make notes about your father's job (or the job of another person in your family). Then think about how you will use your notes to speak.**

5 **Ask and answer in pairs and assess each other's answer.**

1 The information in the answer is *relevant / not relevant*.

2 The answer is *very short / OK / very long*.

3 My partner speaks *with pauses / at normal speed / very fast*.

4 The vocabulary is *relevant / not relevant* to the topic.

5 The pronunciation is *poor / OK / clear*.

6 There are *a lot of errors / one or two errors / no errors* in the grammar.

6 **Read the advice below. Choose one or two pieces of advice to improve your answer. Then ask and answer in pairs again.**

- Give a longer answer. Practise giving answers that are two or three full sentences.
- Imagine you are speaking to a friend and speak at your normal speed – not fast and not slow.

Exam tip

The questions in Part 1 are on general topics about your life. Your answers are from your life and experience. There is no right or wrong answer.

7 **Choose and prepare one more question from Exercise 1. Ask and answer in pairs and assess each other. Then try to improve your answer and practise again.**

Practice for the test

Part 1

1 **Read the questions and record your answers.**

1 Which country are you from?

2 Do you have a large family?

3 What does your mother do?

4 Do you live with your family?

 2 **Listen to three more Part 1 questions. Write the questions. Then record your answers.**

1 ....

2 ....

3 ....

Listening

completing notes • answering multiple-choice questions • completing sentences • labelling diagrams

Get READY for class!

Remember to do your preparation before class.

online • workbook

Develop your exam skills

info

In the Listening test you will hear a group of people talking about a topic related to education or training. You will be asked to do different tasks in this section, and some of these will require you to identify the ideas and opinions of the individual speakers.

Exam tip

In this kind of question, where there are several speakers, it is useful to identify them as early as possible. Listen carefully and write their names on the exam paper, leaving enough room to make a note of any opinions as well.

see **GRAMMAR** page 154 and more **PRACTICE** online

Exam tip

With multiple-choice questions, make sure you read all the options before you choose the answer. Some of the answers may look similar and you should check the details before you decide.

04 1 **You will hear a group of students talking about a project they are planning to present. Choose the correct letter, a, b or c, to complete the sentences.**

1 *'Families' is*
   a the title of the presentation.
   b the topic of the presentation.
   c the name of the course.

2 *Who originally wants to compare families?*
   a Mona
   b Edward
   c Ibrahim

3 *Mandy suggests families from*
   a the Arab Gulf and North Africa.
   b North Africa and South Africa.
   c only Arab countries.

4 *Mona suggests South Africa because*
   a it is big.
   b she knows someone from there.
   c she knows about it herself.

05 2 **Now you will hear the students planning the slides they are going to prepare for their presentation. Listen and complete the notes using NO MORE THAN TWO WORDS OR A NUMBER for each answer.**

Introduction: Families around the world: (1) ....

Total no. of slides: (2) ....

2 slides each, families around the world, including:

How families are (3) .... and how they are (4) ....

Conclusion

06 3 **You will hear two of the students discussing the best way to design a slide. Label the drawing using NO MORE THAN TWO WORDS for each answer.**

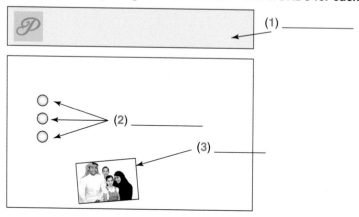

You will hear the four students discussing their presentation. Choose TWO correct answers (a–e).

What do the students have to decide?

a   how to order the slides

b   who will compare the different families

c   the link between North Africa and the US

d   where the Arabs come from originally

e   when Western culture began in the US

Practice for the test

Section 3

 Questions 1–4

You will hear three students talking to their tutor about the presentation they are planning. Choose the correct letter, a, b or c.

1   *The topic of the presentation is*

   a   how mobile phones are designed.

   b   the risks caused by mobile phones.

   c   how mobile phones are used.

2   *The introduction explains*

   a   the dangers of mobile phones.

   b   the importance of mobile phones.

   c   the importance of understanding the dangers of mobile phones.

3   *On the second slide, the students are planning to*

   a   explain why mobile phones are dangerous.

   b   point out some different kinds of risks.

   c   mention ways to avoid the risks.

4   *The tutor suggests*

   a   not discussing the dangers of mobile phones.

   b   discussing the benefits of mobile phones.

   c   having an argument.

 Questions 5–7

Now you will hear the next part of the recording. Listen and complete the slides with ONE WORD ONLY.

Slide 1 Introduction	Slide 2	Slide 3 Introduction
(5)	• Health • (6) .... • Security	(7) .... for avoiding dangers

 Questions 8–10

Now listen to the last part of the recording and complete the sentences. Write NO MORE THAN TWO WORDS OR A NUMBER.

8   The actual talk will last for ....

9   Each student will speak for ....

10   The slides must all have the ....

• identifying information • *True/False/Not given* questions

Get READY for class!

Remember to do your preparation before class.

online • workbook

see **GRAMMAR** page 145 and more **PRACTICE** online

Exam tip

Do not use your own opinion to answer but check in the text.

see **GRAMMAR** page 143 and more **PRACTICE** online

Develop your exam skills

> In the Reading test, you may be asked whether information is correct or not. You will be given a list of statements. If the text confirms the statement, your answer should be 'TRUE'. If the text contradicts the statement, your answer should be 'FALSE'. If it is impossible to know from the text if the statement is true or not, your answer should be 'NOT GIVEN'.

1 Read three statements about families and the questions that follow. Can you answer the questions using only the information in the statements? Put a tick if you can, or write **NOT GIVEN** if not.

Statements	Questions	✓ or NOT GIVEN
Nuclear families, with mother, father and child/children, are more common in large cities.	**1** Can you have a nuclear family of three people?	
	2 Were there any nuclear families 500 years ago?	
In China, there are words for many kinds of family relationships, e.g. a word for 'father's sister's son's daughter's son'.	**3** What is the reason for China having so many words for family relationships?	
	4 Does 'aunt's grandson' have exactly the same meaning as the example?	
One of the main reasons for arranged marriages is to keep money and property in the family.	**5** How does an arranged marriage keep the family money and property safe?	
	6 Are there other reasons for arranged marriages other than keeping wealth in the family?	

2 Read three more statements about families. Write **TRUE** if the text next to it confirms the information, **FALSE** if it contradicts the information, or **NOT GIVEN** if there is not enough information.

Statements	Information	✓ or NOT GIVEN
Children in large families usually don't have many possessions, but one advantage is that they can get help from their brothers and sisters.	**1** Children with lots of brothers and sisters usually have more things of their own.	
	2 Brothers and sisters can provide help for each other.	
	3 Large families share their possessions.	
People sometimes talk about the disadvantages of being a child in a single-parent family, but single parents are often closer to their children.	**4** People think there are many disadvantages of living in a single-parent family.	
	5 Children with one parent are looked after better.	
	6 A single-parent family can have benefits for the children as well as disadvantages.	
In families around the world, the father is usually in charge; however, it is usually the mother who takes charge of the home.	**7** In Britain, the father is usually the head of the family.	
	8 In many countries, although the father is important, the mother deals with the home.	
	9 Mothers are the head of the family in most countries around the world.	

3 Discuss what you have learnt about families in Exercises 1 and 2.

4 Read Part 1 of the text as fast as you can. Try to understand the main idea of what you read even if you do not know all the vocabulary. Check your understanding by answering the questions.

Part 1

Changes in family structure

There are many types of family systems around the world. In North America and northern Europe, the nuclear family (with two generations – a father, mother and one or more children) is often seen as the most typical. In contrast, in most other parts of the world, extended families, which include other family members such as grandparents, aunts, uncles and cousins, are seen as the norm.
True or False? The nuclear family is seen as the most common in the USA.

The common view is that the nuclear family has become the norm in many Western societies as a result of industrialization and urbanization. This trend began in the late eighteenth and nineteenth centuries, when people were forced to move to cities to find work in the factories that sprang up during the Industrial Revolution. In the twentieth century, greater industrialization resulted in even more people leaving their large extended families. Urbanization also meant that people lived in much smaller houses, which were not big enough for an extended family.
True or False? Nuclear families started with the rise in industrialization.

The trend towards nuclear families meant that many of the duties and responsibilities of a family, such as providing food and shelter, cleaning the home, preparing the food, caring for children and their education, and caring for the sick and elderly are no longer shared among the members of the extended family. The parents (or parent) now have to do this, with some help from the state. However, this is the price that people pay for the higher standard of living that may come from living in a city.
True or False? In nuclear families, people have a higher standard of living.

5 Read Part 2 of the text in the same way as you read Part 1 and answer the questions.

Part 2

We may think we know what we mean by a 'nuclear' family and an 'extended' family, but reality is more complicated than most people believe. Most nuclear families are part of extended families: children have grandparents and in many cases, aunts, uncles and cousins as well. Part of what makes them 'nuclear' is that they live in their own separate household, but it is not the whole story. In Greece or Italy, for example, a nuclear family may live in its own flat, but the extended family may live in the same apartment block or in the same street and family members see each other and even eat together every day.
True or False? Nuclear families are isolated from their extended family.

There is at least one more factor to consider. Family members may be separated from each other by geographical distance, but they may have close emotional ties. Even in North America and northern Europe, grandparents usually have close bonds with their grandchildren, and families often travel long distances so that they can see each other. Grandparents often help their adult children, for example, by cooking and looking after their children in emergencies. In the same way, when their parents become too old to live on their own, adult children may take them into their own homes. As a result, they turn their nuclear family into an extended family.
True or False? Members of extended families often look after people who live in other households.

The structure of families changes over time. The effects of urbanization and industrialization are enormous, but they are not the only reasons for the changes. People marry, have children, become widowed, divorce and die. Children grow up and adults grow old. Nuclear families become extended families and extended families become nuclear families. Family ties stay strong or become weak. One thing is certain: in a changing world, the family will continue to change, but ultimately, it is likely to continue to be the basic unit of society.
True, False or Not Given? Changes to family structure will become increasingly fast in the future.

Exam tip

You should adjust your reading speed throughout the exam. When you are looking for detailed information (e.g. the writer's opinion), you will need to slow down to make sure you find the exact answer. When you are asked for more general information, you may be able to skim (e.g. in order to match paragraph headings), or scan (e.g. in order to find a number or detail in the text). By practising, you will find the ideal balance between reading slowly enough to understand and fast enough to finish on time.

Practice for the test

Questions 1–8

Do the following statements agree with the information in the text? Write:

TRUE if the text confirms the statement

FALSE if the text contradicts the statement

NOT GIVEN if it is impossible to know from the text

Statements

1 Sixty years ago, children were expected to help around the house. ....

2 Today the world is a more dangerous place. ....

3 Helicopter parents love their children more than other parents. ....

4 People today have shorter childhoods than children in the past. ....

5 In the past children who lived in the country worked out of doors. ....

6 Eighteenth-century mothers were cruel or indifferent to their children. ....

7 Children serving in the Royal Navy in the eighteenth century might find themselves in charge of adults. ....

8 Modern Western ideas about childhood are probably considered unusual in other cultures. ....

The Meaning of Childhood

What do we mean by a 'normal' childhood? It really depends on the period when a person was born and where they live. If you asked a parent in Britain today, they would probably say that childhood should be the happiest time of a person's life: a time when the child is loved, kept safe and is free to play.

However, even within the same culture, ideas about childhood have changed dramatically within a short period of time. British children growing up in the 1960s or 1970s seem to have had more freedom than children in the early twenty-first century. They were allowed to go about more freely, walking to school or to visit their friends, or using public transport. They were also more likely to be asked to do things like clean floors and wash the dishes and to look after younger brothers and sisters.

Today, parents are far more protective. They worry more about the dangers their children might face, and some parents also involve themselves excessively with their child's experiences and problems. These are the 'helicopter' parents. They are called this because, like helicopters, they continually hover over their child's head.

Childhood also ends later than it used to. At the beginning of the twentieth century, a twelve-year-old girl might have been sent off to work in a factory or as a maid for a wealthy family. She would have earned money and sent some of it back to her family. Twelve-year-old boys often become apprentices and learnt a trade, and in the countryside children worked in the fields and looked after animals almost as soon as they could walk.

The further back we go in history, the more difficult it is to have an accurate picture of attitudes to childhood. We know very little, for example, about the attitudes of mothers in eighteenth-century Britain. For example, what sort of mother could send her son, still a child, to join the Royal Navy, where he could expect a tough life, bad food and constant danger? Was she indifferent, cruel, or did she simply have no choice? And yet, boys as young as ten were sent away to sea. And it wasn't only the sons of the poor; wealthy families sent their sons, some as young as eight, to join the navy. Incredibly, they were put in charge of men who had many years of experience at sea.

So how have things changed? In some societies people are having fewer children. Does this fact alone mean that children are more precious to their parents and that therefore they have more of a 'normal' childhood? There is a concern that in a family with an only child, the parents and grandparents give the child a huge amount of attention and spoil them by buying them anything the child wants. The result of this is that the child expects their parents to do anything they tell them to, which creates problems for the child as they start to grow up.

A childhood in the slums of Bangladesh or on the war-torn streets of so many parts of the world remains what it has been for most children for much of history: a time of physical hardship, danger and little opportunity to get an education.

Writing

Structuring a Task 2 opinion essay

Get READY for class!

Remember to do your preparation before class.

online • workbook

Develop your exam skills

> **info**
>
> Task 2 in the IELTS exam asks a question about a social topic such as the environment, education or the media. You must answer this question by giving your opinions, along with reasons and examples, in an essay. You must write at least 250 words and you should spend about 40 minutes writing the essay.
>
> It is important to use a standard essay structure consisting of separate paragraphs: an introduction (one paragraph), followed by the main body of the essay (two or three paragraphs), and then a conclusion (one paragraph).

see **GRAMMAR** page 157 and more **PRACTICE** online

1 **Read about one view of parenting. Do you agree or disagree with the author? Then read about how the paragraph is structured below.**

I believe ¹the family is one of the most important structures in society. ²Within the family, children can learn how to get on with other people and how to behave, and these things are important for life in the wider world. The family should also be a stable unit that ³provides children with love and support. Without this love and support, children might find it difficult to manage in the wider world. For example, children without loving, supportive parents could feel unable to do the things they would like to do, like go to university.

1 Main idea: *The family is important.*

2 Supporting idea which explains/adds to main idea: People *learn how to get on with others and how to behave in a family.*

3 Supporting idea: *The family gives love and support.*

Circled words = use of cautious language

2 **Read the following statements and write T (True) or F (False).**

1 A paragraph should have more than one *main idea.* ....

2 A paragraph should have more than one *supporting idea.* ....

3 The first sentence of a paragraph should contain the *main idea* of the paragraph.

   ....

4 The last sentence of a paragraph should contain the *main idea* of the paragraph.

   ....

5 You should mainly use definite modal verbs, e.g. *will, must.* ....

6 You should mainly use less definite modal verbs, e.g. *can, might, could, should.*

   ....

see **GRAMMAR** pages 147 and 157 and more **PRACTICE** online

3 **Now read the following three paragraphs. Decide which one follows the rules in Exercise 1. Discuss with a partner what is wrong with the other two.**

Paragraph A: Children should learn rules from their parents because teachers alone cannot teach a child how to behave. If a child doesn't have to obey strict rules at home, they could ignore the rules of the school and behave badly. Parents should teach a child rules from an early age so that when they reach school age they are more likely to behave and make friends with the other children at school.

Paragraph B: Children will be really terrible if they have terrible parents. For example, some children in my school misbehave but their parents don't care; although the teacher complains to the parents, the parents don't do anything about it. It is better for children if their parents teach them rules from an early age because then the child will behave better. Rules must be taught by parents and teachers.

Paragraph C: Rules are important and must be taught by both parents and teachers. Rules need to be taught by parents first because this will help when the child gets into school. If a child is not taught to follow rules, he or she will misbehave. Furthermore, morals also need to be taught by parents. A child needs to learn the difference between right and wrong from their parents. Parents should also teach a child social skills, whereas the teacher's job is to teach them school subjects.

> **Exam tip**
>
> An essay should be made up of separate paragraphs, and the points within each paragraph should follow a logical order: a main idea followed by supporting ideas which explain or add to the main idea.

4 **Read the first paragraph below. Look at how the first sentence summarizes what follows. Complete the first line of the following three paragraphs in the same way.**

1   _Family structures are changing in the West._

Once, the traditional family structure of two parents with two children was the most common family type in Western countries like the UK and the USA but this is changing. New family structures include single-parent families and families with children from more than one marriage. These new family types are becoming increasingly common. Different family structures mean that many children live with various combinations of full, step- or half-brothers and sisters.

2   ....

If more women go out to work, this could affect the children in the family because they are not receiving the attention they need. Many people claim that children are happy when both their parents are working, but someone needs to look after the children and the home, and in my opinion, women are often better at this role than men.

3   ....

Having brothers and sisters means that a child learns how to socialize with other children from a young age and this is incredibly beneficial for them. They also grow up and grow old with an existing support network around them, which people with no brothers and sisters may not have. An only child can also be very lonely.

4   ....

It is not a child's job to cook, clean or help in the home. Children should be playing and having fun because childhood is the only time when they will be free from work. They should be developing rather than becoming tired doing housework. Although many argue that helping in the home teaches children to look after their environment and to be clean, children don't need to do housework to learn these things.

5 **Read the essay question and think about what you would expect to read in the essay. Then read the essay on page 15 and put the paragraphs in the correct order by matching them to the headings.**

In a family, both men and women should be employed outside the home and share childcare equally. To what extent do you agree with this statement?

a I believe that men should work outside the home and women should not because of the undoubted benefits for the family as a whole. These traditional roles have worked successfully for a long time so, in my opinion, they do not need to change now.

b I also believe women should be the main carers for their children. Although some people argue that women should be able to work outside the home, this is hard when there are children. Women need to be with their children when they are babies, and it is also better for young children to grow up with a parent who is always at home. It is not good for children to be looked after a professional carer.

c Nowadays, the traditional roles of men and women have changed. More men help in the home and more women go out to work. Some people say that this is a good thing, while others say that this is a negative thing. I believe that men should go out to work and women should stay at home because this is more economically efficient and it is also better for children.

d There are more economic benefits for a family with a traditional family structure where the man works and the woman stays at home. A man working full time is likely to earn more money than a man and woman who both work part time. A further benefit is that the woman can do things at home to save money, like making clothes or growing food.

Paragraph 1 (Introduction): ....

Paragraph 2: ....

Paragraph 3: ....

Paragraph 4 (Conclusion): ....

6 **Now match the parts of an essay to their functions.**

1 Introduction ....

2 Main body ....

3 Conclusion ....

a Gives some general information about the essay topic, may put forward some differing opinions and gives an answer to the essay question.

b Summarizes all the arguments and restates your answer/opinion.

c Describes and explains different viewpoints, arguments, advantages and disadvantages, supported by examples.

Exam tip

The introduction to a Task 2 essay can describe the topic of the essay, give background information to it and list various opinions about it. You should also briefly state your own view, which you then go on to explain and support in the main body of the essay.

Practice for the test

Task 2

You should spend about 40 minutes on this task.

Write about the following topic:

Children should always follow their parents' advice.

To what extent do you agree or disagree with this statement?

Give reasons for your answer and include any relevant examples from your own knowledge or experience.

Write at least 175 words.

Unit 2

Leisure

Listening

completing forms and tables • answering multiple-choice questions

Develop your exam skills

Exam tip

Some words can be confused because two letters may sound similar, for example: *p* and *b*, *l* and *r*. If you find these tricky, make sure you get plenty of practice distinguishing between them before the exam.

🎧 11 **1** Say the ten pairs of words quietly to yourself to prepare for the listening. Then listen to the recording and circle the word you hear. You will hear the words twice.

1 fly / fry   6 play / pray
2 play / pray   7 lead / read
3 lead / read   8 fly / fry
4 blade / played   9 blade / played
5 collect / correct   10 collect / correct

🎧 12 **2** You will hear two people discussing their hobbies. Listen and circle the words you hear.

1 flying / frying / fly in   3 leading / reading / lead in
2 play / played / blade

> **info**
>
> In this type of task, you will have to complete a table with information from the recording. Before you listen, read the headings of the columns in the table to see what kind of information you need to listen for. Remember to keep to the word count.

3 The table below shows how one person keeps a record of the stamps in their collection. Discuss with a partner what kind of stamps a collector might look for. Then think about the kind of information that should go under each heading, e.g. a number, a name or a date.

Value	Picture	Year	Origin
(1)	(2) *colour, image*	(3)	(4) ....

see GRAMMAR
page 145 and more
PRACTICE online

 4 You will hear a student talking to a friend about his stamp collection. Listen and complete the table about his stamps. Write **NO MORE THAN TWO WORDS OR A NUMBER.** Did the preparation in Exercise 3 help you with the listening task?

Value	Picture	Year	Origin
32 cents	cardinal honeyeater	(1)	(2) ....
25 cents	parrot	(3)	(4) ....

Exam tip

In this type of IELTS task you will often need to listen for numbers and letters. These might be part of an address, a name, an age or a phone number. Before you listen, read the task carefully. It will give you a lot of clues about the topic of the recording and the kind of information you will need.

5 Read the questions that a student has to answer when applying to join a mountain climbing club. Check your understanding of the questions. Then make a note of the kind of information needed to answer the questions.

Question	Type of information
1 Are you over 18?	*age* ....
2 Where do you live?	....
3 What's your family name?	....
4 Do you have a number where I can contact you?	....
5 Do you have any health problems?	....
6 Do you have any climbing experience?	....

 6 You will now hear the student talking to an administrator of a climbing club. Check your understanding of the application form. Then listen and complete it.

Mountain High Climbing Club

Membership Application Form

Name: (1) ....

Age: (2) ....

Address: (3) .... Highbury Square, LONDON, W1

Telephone number: (4) 07209 ....

Health problems: None

Previous experience: (*circle one*) (5) *none / some / extensive*

Practice for the test

Section 1

 Questions 1–4

You will hear two students talking about university clubs and societies. Listen and complete the table. Write NO MORE THAN TWO WORDS OR A NUMBER.

Club	Membership fee	Number of members
(1)	£20	60
cross country cycling	£15	(2) ....
film and drama	£50	(3) ....
(4)	£5	80

 Questions 5–7

Now you will hear the next part of the recording. Choose THREE letters, a–g.

Which THREE activities does Victoria enjoy?

a	contemporary dance	**e**	photography
b	yoga	**f**	running
c	film and drama	**g**	jazz and tap dancing
d	cycling		

5 ....   6 ....   7 ....

 Questions 8–10

Now listen to the last part of the recording and complete the form. Write NO MORE THAN TWO WORDS OR A NUMBER.

Club Membership Application Form

(tick relevant clubs)

athletics	☐	cycling	☐	running	☐	table tennis	☐
baseball	☐	kick boxing	☐	sailing	☐	yoga	☐
basketball	☐	parachuting	☐	snooker	☐		
chess	☐	photography	☐	street dance	☐		
contemporary dance	☐	pilates	☐	swimming	☐		

Name: Victoria (8) ....

Age: 19

Address: (9) 57, ... , Atherton Park, Manchester, M46

Contact number: (10) ....

Email: victoriainatherton@england.com

Speaking

expressing preferences • present simple • identifying key words in discussion

Get READY for class!

Remember to do your preparation before class.

online • workbook

Develop your exam skills

The complete Speaking test (Parts 1, 2 and 3) takes 11–14 minutes. The examiner asks questions and the candidate gives answers. The answers are recorded.

Part 2: Individual long turn

- Part 2 takes 3–4 minutes.
- The examiner gives you a 'task card' with written prompts. He/She asks you to talk about the topic and include the points on the card. The topic is about a personal experience.
- You have one minute to prepare your talk and the examiner gives you a pencil and paper to make notes.
- You talk for one to two minutes about the topic. You can use your notes to help you.
- Then the examiner asks you one or two more questions on the same topic.
- Part 2 tests your ability to talk and develop your ideas about a topic using relevant vocabulary and grammar. It also tests your ability to give a fluent and organized answer.

info

18 **1** Read the task card and decide how you would answer. Do you think the task is easy or difficult? Then listen to the examiner's instructions. What extra information does he give?

> **Describe a <u>newspaper or magazine</u> you enjoy reading.**
>
> You should say:
>
> <u>what kind</u> of newspaper or magazine it is
> <u>which parts</u> of it you read
> <u>when</u> and <u>where</u> you read it
>
> and <u>explain why</u> you enjoy reading it.

Exam tip

It is very useful to identify 'key words' in exam questions and exam information. These are important words which show you what to include in your answer.

see **GRAMMAR** page 143 and more **PRACTICE** online

19 **2** Look at the underlined key words on the task card in Exercise 1 above. Then read the notes on each key word below. Listen to the student's answer and circle the notes that she talks about.

1 newspaper or magazine: magazine | newspaper
2 what kind: fashion | sport | travel
3 which parts: adverts | interviews | letters | news
4 when: every day | the weekend | sometimes
5 where: home | school
6 explain why: It's very interesting. | It's relaxing.

3 Match the sentences below to the key words in Exercise 2. Then listen again and check. Think of any follow-up questions you could ask, for example: *Who are your favourite players?*

a I enjoy reading a magazine called *Fab Football*. *newspaper and magazine*

b I prefer reading the interviews with famous players or the news. ....

c I read *Fab Football* every weekend. ....

d It's about sport. ....

e It's very interesting. ....

f Then I go home and read. ....

4 Make your own notes for the task card in Exercise 1 using the key words to help you.

1 newspaper or magazine: ....

2 what kind: ....

3 which parts: ....

4 when: ....

5 where: ....

7 explain why: ....

5 Expand your notes from Exercise 4 to make sentences.

1 newspaper or magazine: ....

2 what kind: ....

3 which parts: ....

4 when: ....

5 where: ....

6 explain why: ....

Practice for the test

Part 2

1 Read the task card below and listen to the examiner's instructions. Underline the key words.

> **Describe an activity you like doing.**
>
> You should say:
>
> what activity it is
> where and when you do it
> who you like doing it with
>
> and explain why you enjoy doing it.

2 Plan your answer. Write notes for each of the key words. You have one minute for this in the exam.

3 Record your answer. You have one to two minutes for this in the exam.

Answering multiple-choice questions

Develop your exam skills

In the exam, there are different types of multiple-choice questions: you may be asked to choose the correct answer to a question, or you may be given a choice of sentence endings and asked to form a sentence that reflects the meaning of the text. The questions will be in the same order as the information in the text.

1 Discuss in groups what you find difficult about answering multiple-choice questions and ways of making it easier. Then read the text for general understanding and answer the question:
How important is friendship for teenagers?

The value of friendship

Recent research into the world of teenagers has suggested that they value friendship above everything else. Children aged between 12 and 15 were asked what was important to them. Their answers included possessions such as money and computer gadgets but also relationships with people.

The teenagers questioned said that friends were the most important to them, more important even than family or boyfriends and girlfriends. We wanted to find out more about the results of this research so we asked our readers what they thought about the value of friendship. Here are some examples of what they said about their friends.

Ben, 15

Every time I have a fight with my parents, I need some time on my own. But after that, the first thing I do is meet up with my friends. After playing football for a while or skateboarding, I usually feel much happier again.

Rory, 13

When I moved to a village in the countryside, I thought that it would be the end of my friendships. But my old friends have kept in touch and they come and visit in the holidays. There's a lake nearby, so we often go sailing, water-skiing or windsurfing. And I have made some new friends here at school since I joined the rugby club.

Carlos, 11

Last year, I broke my arm on a skiing holiday. Unfortunately, it was my left arm and I am left-handed. My school friends all helped and copied their notes for me.

It seems that our readers value their friendships very highly. From what they told us, they spend a lot of time with their friends, just hanging out or sharing hobbies and interests. They seem to need their friends for advice, help, chats and for having fun. Clearly, friends make each other feel better. Looking at what our readers told us, the results of the recent research are not really surprising.

2 Read the options below and choose the best answer. Defend your choice by explaining it to others in your group. Check your answer on page 00.

To teenagers, money is

a not important.

b as important as computer gadgets.

c as important as relationships with people.

d less important than friendships.

Exam tip

Finding the key words in a question – the most important words – can help you locate the relevant section of the text more quickly.

see **GRAMMAR** page 145 and get more **PRACTICE** online

Exam tip

If a question is difficult, don't spend too much time on it; go on to the next one. Once you find the next answer, you can go back in the text to find the answer to the previous question. This is because in this type of task, the questions are in the same order as the information in the text.

3 Read the multiple-choice questions without their answer options. Underline the question words (e.g. *where, when, what*) and the key words in each of the questions (1–3) and sentence stems (4–5).

1 Why are Ben, Rory and Carlos mentioned in the article?
2 Which of the following best describes Ben?
3 What do we know about the lake that Rory visits?
4 Carlos mentions that he is left-handed because …
5 The answers to the recent research and the answers from the readers …

4 Read the multiple-choice questions and the options and choose the best answer, a, b, c or d. Did Exercise 3 help you make the right choice?

1 *Why are Ben, Rory and Carlos mentioned in the article?*
  a They know why teenagers value friendship.
  b They give information about themselves.
  c They read magazines.
  d They are teenage boys.

2 *Which of the following best describes Ben?*
  a He often has fights.
  b He likes being alone.
  c He is happier than his friends.
  d He likes some sports.

3 *What do we know about the lake that Rory visits?*
  a It is near the school.
  b It is near his home.
  c It is used by a lot of people who do water sports.
  d It is in a village.

4 *Carlos mentions that he is left-handed because*
  a it makes skiing harder.
  b it makes it worse that he broke the arm he uses most.
  c it is an interesting fact about himself.
  d it is very unfortunate when you break your left arm.

5 *The answers to the recent research and the answers from the readers*
  a were surprising.
  b were the same.
  c were similar.
  d were both about sports.

Practice for the test

Questions 1–6

Choose the correct letter, a, b, c or d.

1 **How many friends do the majority of people probably have?**
  a 30 real friends or fewer
  b a minimum of 30 real friends
  c 150 Internet friends
  d 400 Internet friends over the course of their lives

2 **It is difficult**
  a to believe the numbers about friendship.
  b to keep your friends happy.
  c to trust what you read on social networking sites.
  d to give a definition of friendship.

3 **Friendship means**

    a different things to different people.

    b dying for your friends if you need to.

    c helping each other until it is no longer necessary.

    d accepting people with different views.

4 **Sometimes people worry because**

    a they think that they have too many friends.

    b they spend too much time with friends.

    c they think they are too old to make friends.

    d there are no guidelines about friendship.

5 **Most of us**

    a are dissatisfied with our friends.

    b build friendships late in life.

    c are frightened to talk to strangers.

    d need to be with others.

6 **What does 'Strangers are friends we have not met yet' mean?**

    a We have not met strangers before.

    b Strangers are also our friends.

    c We should not talk to strangers.

    d Strangers may become our friends.

It is said that most people have no more than 30 friends at any given time, and 400 over the whole of their lives. However, on social networking sites, most users have about 150 friends. If these numbers are correct, then friendship means different things in different situations.

One of the reasons people have more online friends than real friends at any particular point in time is that online friendships do not require much time and energy: it is easy to make Internet friends and keep them forever. Another possibility is that it is difficult to say 'no' when somebody asks us to be their friend online, even if we feel we don't really know them. The fact that they ask us suggests that they do consider us a friend, which is a nice feeling. Alternatively, they may be 'collectors' of online friends and simply want to use us to get a higher number of friends and appear to be popular.

Online friendships are quite easy, but in the real world things are much more difficult. There are no rules about friendship. There are no guidelines about how to make friends, how to keep friendships going, and how to finish friendships if we want to move on. People also have very different opinions about friendship: some people would die for their friends and value them more than family. Others feel that friends are temporary, only there to help each other until they are no longer needed. If people with such different views become friends, this can lead to problems.

Because of these different definitions of friendship, it is easy to be unhappy about our friends. We may want our relationship with them to be deeper or closer, or we may want to have more friends in our lives. Sometimes we simply do not have the time to develop our friendships, or we fear we have left it too late in life to start. If we move to another country or city, we have to find ways to make new friends again.

This dissatisfaction shows us how important friendships are for most of us. We should not think that it could be too late to build new friendships. We also need to understand that the need to be around others is shared by many people. Therefore, we should not be too frightened to start talking to people who may become our friends in the future: it is likely that they too would like to get closer to us. Remember what people say: strangers are friends we have not met yet.

Answer to Exercise 2: The correct answer is **d**. The teenagers said that money, gadgets and relationships are all important to them. However, the text also tells us that the teenagers value friendships most, therefore money is less important.

Develop your exam skills

> In Task 1, you need to describe visual information, e.g. the information in a table. You need to identify and describe the key points using formal or semi-formal language. You have 20 minutes to do this task and you must write 150 words or more.

1 **Look at the table below. Write T (True) or F (False) next to each sentence. Think about your reasons for each choice.**

Number of hours a week spent on activities by age range					
Age range	Football	Swimming	Television	Computer games	Music
13–15 years	5	2	6	7	3
16–18 years	4	1.5	9	14	12

1 Older teenagers spend a lot of time swimming. ____F____

2 Listening to music is more popular with older teenagers. ....

3 Teenagers don't spend much time swimming. ....

4 Younger teenagers spend a lot of hours listening to music. ....

2 **Look at the table below. Choose the sentence, a, b or c, which best explains what the table shows.**

% of time spent on types of Internet activity, by age group					
Age group	Shopping	Social networking	Browsing news sites	Browsing sports sites	Playing games
10–15 years	0	23	2	5	70
16–20 years	10	51	8	10	21
21–29 years	24	44	8	6	16
30–39 years	35	25	16	14	10
40–49 years	29	10	30	19	2
50+ years	10	5	54	23	1

a The table shows how much time people spend on the Internet.

b The table shows how much time they spend on Internet activities depending on age.

c The table shows the percentage of time spent on types of Internet activity by age group.

Exam tip

Make sure you understand the following in a table:

• the main heading / the title of the table

• the column headings / categories and exactly what these show

Look for the most important information in the table by comparing categories and groups. Notice any similarities, any differences, any obvious changes and / or trends. These are what you will need to write about in your answer.

3 Read two introductions, A and B, to a text about the table in Exercise 2 and answer the questions.

1 Circle all the verbs in the introductions. What tense are the verbs?
2 Does the first sentence in each introduction accurately explain the table title?
3 Underline any details in A and B.
4 Which introduction is better, A or B? Why?

Introduction A: The table shows how much time different age groups spend on five types of Internet activity. There are six age ranges in the table, from 10–15 to over 50. The Internet activities include shopping, browsing, social networking and playing games.

Introduction B: The table shows how much people like the Internet depending on their age. 70% of children aged 10–15 play games on the Internet but no children aged 10–15 like shopping. Most older people browse news sites. They spend 54% of their time reading Internet news.

Exam tip

Use the following structure for the introduction to a Task 1 answer:

- One sentence to explain what the table shows. (Use different words from the words used in the heading for the table wherever possible.)
- One or two sentences summarizing the information shown in the table.
- Do not include details in the introduction. Save the details for the main part of your text, after the introduction.

see GRAMMAR pages 151 and 152 and get more PRACTICE online

4 Read the rest of the text about the table. Complete the text using the words, phrases or numbers below.

> 16–20   younger age groups   10–15
> shopping   older   like   much   No

In general, there are many differences depending on age group. The table shows that
(1) .... spend a lot of time playing games but older people
do not spend (2) .... time playing games. Younger people
spend more time social networking than older people, especially the age range
(3) .... They spend 51% of their time social networking.
Most age groups shop on the Internet with the exception of those in the age group
(4) .... (5) .... people in this
age group shop on the Internet. Browsing news and sports sites is popular with
(6) .... age groups. Overall, young people like playing
games and social networking but older people (7) ....
reading the news and (8) .... on the Internet.

Practice for the test

Task 1
You should spend about 20 minutes on this task.

The table below shows the television viewing figures for sports by country, in millions.

Summarize the information by selecting and reporting the main features, and make comparisons where relevant.

Write at least 100 words.

Exam tip

Always use the present tense to describe a table unless it contains information about a time in the past or if past dates, e.g. years, are used as categories.

Television viewing figures for sports by country, in millions					
Country	Tennis	Golf	Motor racing	Athletics	Totals
Australia	6.2	4.5	3.7	3	17.4
UK	6.6	2.8	6.4	4.5	20.3
USA	7	11.2	1.5	5.5	25.2
Canada	6.1	3.4	1.1	3.9	14.5
Total	25.9	21.9	12.7	16.9	

Unit 3

Different cultures

connecting ideas • past simple • pronunciation: verbs ending in -ed • giving long answers

Get READY for class!

Remember to do your preparation before class.

online • workbook

Develop your exam skills

The complete Speaking test (Parts 1, 2 and 3) takes 11–14 minutes. The examiner asks questions and the candidate gives answers. The answers are recorded.

Part 3: Two-way discussion

- Part 3 takes 4–5 minutes.
- The questions in Part 3 relate to the topic in Part 2.
- The discussion is between the examiner and you.
- The examiner asks you questions. You talk about different issues and ideas on the topic.
- Part 3 tests your ability to talk about other topics related to the Part 2 topic and to express and justify your personal opinions and ideas.

1 Look at the beginnings of Part 2 task cards 1–3. Match each card with a general topic a–c. Which topic would you find easiest to answer and why?

1
Describe someone in your family who you like.

You should say:

what kind of person he/she is

2
Describe an activity that you like doing.

You should say:

what activity it is

3
Describe a special occasion in your life.

You should say:

where this occasion took place

a events ....

b hobbies ....

c people ....

Exam tip

The Part 2 task prepares you for Part 3 because you talk about a related topic.

2 Look at three typical questions from Part 3. Match each question a–c with a task card 1–3 from Exercise 1. Ask and answer each question.

a Do young people in your country celebrate special occasions? ....

b What do you think are the differences between sports now and in the past? ....

c What is the role of grandparents in your culture? ....

4 Look at the underlined key words in the Part 3 question below. Listen to two more Part 3 questions. Write the questions and underline the key words. Then listen again and check.

Do <u>you think</u> <u>computer</u> <u>games</u> are good?

1 ....

2 ....

Read answers from two different students to one of the questions in Exercise 3. Which question do the answers match?

Student A

Yes, I think, yes. In my country, we have one or two big festivals. And ... um ... also we visit family or we remember people or events. I think it's important. I mean, it's a serious thing but it's fun. I like travelling to other countries for festivals too. It's interesting to learn about the world.

Student B

I went to a festival in my country last year and I enjoyed it. It was important to me because I saw my friends and family.

see **GRAMMAR** page 147 and more **PRACTICE** online

Exam tip

Try to give an answer of four or more sentences. Do not give short answers.

5 Read the students' answers again. Answer the questions about each one.

1 Is the answer on the same general topic?

2 Is it relevant to the question?

3 Does it include the key words or words similar to the key words?

6 In Exercise 4, what three phrases does Student A use to help link ideas?

7 Choose a Part 3 question from Exercise 2 or Exercise 3 and write your own answer. Record your answer. Then assess it using the questions in Exercise 5.

Practice for the test

Part 2

1 Read the Part 2 task card and write notes for your answer. You have one minute for this in the exam.

Describe a special occasion in your life.

You should say:

where this occasion took place
when it took place
who was there

and describe how you felt on this occasion.

2 Record your answer. You have one to two minutes for this in the exam.

Part 3

 3 Read and listen to the Part 3 questions.

What is an important festival in your country?

What are your favourite parts of this festival?

How have special occasions such as weddings changed in your country?

4 Record your answers to each question in Exercise 3.

Reading

Get READY for class!

Remember to do your preparation before class.

online • workbook

Develop your exam skills

info

In the exam, you may be given a list of headings and a text divided into sections. The headings will be in the form of short statements which summarize the information in a section. You will need to read the text sections quickly (using a skimming technique) and decide which of the headings best fits that section. This type of task tests whether you understand the organization of texts and can identify the main idea or topic in a paragraph.

1 Read paragraph A on page 29 and identify the main point of the paragraph. Look for the phrase that gives information about what the text will be about and <u>underline</u> it.

2 Read paragraphs B–D and identify links to the main paragraph. <u>Underline</u> any evidence that shows that comparing styles across countries is difficult. Notice how one main theme is developed throughout the text.

see **GRAMMAR** page 159 and get more **PRACTICE** online

3 Identify the following phrases in the text. Then think about how they relate to the overall theme of 'the difficulty of making comparisons'. The first one is done for you.

moreover (in A): introduces another reason why it is difficult to compare styles/periods

first of all (in B)	secondly (in B)	despite (in C)
then again (in C)	moreover (in C)	unsurprisingly (in D)

4 Read paragraphs B–D again and find examples of particular periods. Do you think these examples help clarify the general theme?

5 Look at the following suggestions for a conclusion of this text and cross out any that are not suitable. The conclusion could:

a highlight the point about how easy it is to be confused (i.e. the fact that different words refer to the same period and that the same words can refer to different periods)

b refer back to the three main examples in paragraphs A–D

c mention that non-British people may find it harder to understand the vocabulary relating to artistic styles

d give information about another period (e.g. introduce the Elizabethan period)

e include a personal opinion or comment relating to the main idea or its consequences (e.g. visitors to the UK may need more information about tourist attractions than we might think).

A It is not easy to compare the artistic styles and periods of different countries. This is partly because they may use different words to refer to the same features, or even use the same words with a slightly different meaning. Moreover, particular styles and periods overlap.

B An example of this is the 'Victorian' period in Britain, which has a style that is often described as romantic. First of all, the name of this period links it immediately with British royal history, which could create confusion to non-British people who know little about it – Queen Victoria's reign lasted from 1837 until her death in 1901. Secondly, the Victorian style itself continued right into the twentieth century, and it could also be argued that there are different styles that can be called Victorian, for example, the use of flower patterns and pastel colours.

C Despite Victorian times being characterized by romanticism, the famous British romantic poets belong to the period before Queen Victoria. These are poets such as Robert Burns, William Wordsworth, Samuel Taylor Coleridge and John Keats. There are also famous writers from the same period, such as Jane Austen and Mary Shelley (the author of *Frankenstein*), and great architects, such as James Wyatt and John Nash. The great painters Gainsborough, Reynolds, Turner and Constable also belong to the pre-Victorian period. But who outside of Britain could label this era? And even if we know they can all be described as Georgian artists, which King George does this refer to? Actually, it refers to four of them (George I, George II, George III and George IV), covering a long period including most of the eighteenth century and some of the nineteenth. But then again, there was a Georgian revival in the twentieth century. Moreover, the style itself incorporates previous styles, including gothic; it also has its own subdivision, Regency style, which describes the period of George IV.

D The period after the Victorian era is referred to as Edwardian, after Edward VII, who reigned from 1901 to 1910, when he died. Unsurprisingly, nobody is sure whether 1910 is the correct end point for the period. Some people suggest it should be 1912, when the Titanic sank, the start of World War I (1914), its end (1918), or the signing of the post-war peace treaty of Versailles (1919). And then, in other European countries the Art Nouveau era ended around the same time …

Practice for the test

1 The reading passage has five sections, A–F. Choose the correct heading for sections A–F from the list of numbered headings below. Write the correct number 1–10 next to sections A–F.

List of headings

1 The disappearance of traditional playground sports

2 The disappearance of classic playground games

3 The dangers of the playground

4 The best traditional games in Britain

5 Possible explanations for the bans

6 Not a very British bulldog

7 No real support for the bans

8 Differing opinions about the bans

9 Different ways of playing

10 A closer look at some traditional games

Sections

Section A: ....

Section B: ....

Section C: ....

Section D: ....

Section E: ....

Section F: ....

Is this the end of traditional British playground pastimes?

Section A

A survey has suggested that traditional pastimes are increasingly being banned at break times in primary schools. Number one on the list is the chasing game British Bulldog, followed by leapfrog and conkers.

Section B

Despite its name, British Bulldog is a game that does not involve animals, and is played all over the world in a number of variations. In its basic form it involves runners trying to get to the other side of the playground without being caught by the chaser, the 'bulldog'. If caught, they become a bulldog too, until there is only one person left: the winner of the game. 'Conkers', on the other hand, is genuinely British as it is a game that was invented in England. The players bring their own 'conker' – a horse chestnut attached to a thick piece of string that goes through the middle of the nut and is knotted underneath. Players pair up, wrap the string around one of their hands and try up to three times to hit the other person's conker by swinging the conker back and forth. They take turns doing this until one of the conkers is destroyed. That could be the end of the game or the winner could go on to play against others. There are different types of scoring methods in place. The game is also played outside the school playground, with a world championship taking place in England every year.

Section C

It will come as no surprise that people have had accidents resulting in a broken arm or leg while playing British Bulldog, or simply while walking across the playground when a game was taking place! It is also not difficult to imagine that many conker players manage to hit their opponent's hand rather than their conker. Horse chestnuts are very hard and being hit with one hurts, as many school children will tell you proudly.

Section D

Banning games is not something new. In the past, we have heard stories about schools banning tig and musical chairs. There is also anecdotal evidence that some schools have banned marbles and even hopscotch, duck-duck-goose and skipping. The main reason for forbidding these games is the fear of injury. Sometimes the justifications given for the ban are strange and perhaps not actually true. For example, tig, a chase game where the chaser catches a person by touching them (who then in turn becomes the chaser), may pass on germs. And conkers might also be a problem for children with nut allergies.

Section E

Sporting activities are also becoming rarer in the playground, often because there is a lack of staff available to supervise them. Apart from banning these, there are also more original solutions, such as allowing students to play touch rugby only – a form of rugby where tackles are not allowed – and playing football with a soft ball rather than the traditional leather one. Having said that, these activities are often not popular with children, and this may discourage them from playing the traditional versions.

Section F

Your comments:

This is just ridiculous! Illnesses and injuries are part of growing up! *Sean, Watford*

I used to play all these games, and more. I think I split my lip once when I fell over during a circle game, but so what? It can't compare with the hours of fun I had with my friends. *Susan, Bournemouth*

I don't think it's wrong to question whether we should allow violent games in schools. After all, violence should not be tolerated in an educational environment. Perhaps this could lead to healthy group discussions involving teachers and pupils about rules and behaviour, but at the same time, it should not result in banning healthy running games such as circle, tag or chase games. Otherwise all P.E. and sports activities should also be banned on health and safety grounds, which would be mad. *Kiran, Cardiff*

Let's ban active playground activities. Let's keep kids inside classrooms during break times and pay extra staff to supervise them and keep them safe. Let's watch them become fat and very boring adults! *A. Watson, Sheffield*

Allowing children to play games that involve the occasional risk, such as British Bulldog, teaches them to make intelligent decisions about their safety. *Mohammed, Scotland*

Glossary

leapfrog: a game that children play, in which a child bends over, while others jump over their back. • *horse chestnut:* the nut of a horse chestnut tree (a large tree which has leaves with several pointed parts and shiny reddish-brown nuts) • *marbles:* a children's game played with small balls, usually made of coloured glass, in which you roll a ball along the ground and try to hit an opponent's ball

Listening

matching sentence endings • answering short-answer questions • answering multiple-choice questions

Get READY for class!

Remember to do your preparation before class.

online • workbook

see GRAMMAR
page 151and more
PRACTICE online

Exam tip

When listening for comparisons and contrasts, *compare* means to look at things to see how they are similar and how they are different; *contrast* means to look at things to see how they are different.

see GRAMMAR
page 151and more
PRACTICE online

Develop your exam skills

1 You will hear a conversation between a tutor and a student about a project on how much people talk in public in different countries. Underline the comparing and contrasting words you hear.

> the same as   different from   more [adjective] than   much more [adjective]
> in comparison with   [adjective] -er than   like

We often use other words with comparisons to emphasize or limit any similarity. For example: 'The pronunciation of the Spanish language in South America is <u>not exactly the same as</u> the pronunciation of Spanish in Spain.' This is the same as: 'The pronunciation of the Spanish language in South America <u>is similar in some ways</u> to the pronunciation of Spanish in Spain, <u>but not in other ways</u>.'

2 **Complete the table with the words below. The first one has been done for you.**

> ~~very~~   a bit   extremely   incredibly
> quite   not   a little   exactly   rather

To emphasize similarity	To limit similarity
very	

We also use words like *and*, *as well as* and *too* to show that things are similar.

Rice is popular in India <u>as well as</u> in China.

Rice is popular in India and in China, <u>too</u>.

We use words like *but*, *except* and *apart from* to show that things are different.
Most houses in the UK are made of brick <u>but</u> blocks of flats are made of concrete.
Many homes in the UK are made of brick, <u>except / apart from</u> blocks of flats, which are made of concrete.

 3 **You will hear three people discussing eating habits in their home countries. Listen carefully for the relevant part of the conversation. Choose THREE letters, a–g.**

Match the country where they eat this food for lunch.

a potatoes	d noodle soup	g chicken
b cereal, toast and eggs	e rice and vegetables	
c bread with lentils	f a sandwich	

1 in the UK .... **2** in India .... **3** in China ....

Exam tip

In this type of multiple-choice question, try turning the first half of the sentence – the sentence stem – into a question. It might help you find the right answer.

 4 **Read the sentence stems and make them into questions.**

1 In traditional Indian families the bride and groom meet for the first time at …

....

2 In India the father of the bride used to …

....

3 Recently it has become very popular for Indian families to …

....

4 After they are married, the couple live …

....

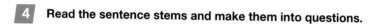 **5** **You will hear two students comparing marriage customs in their countries. Read the statements below. Then listen and choose the correct answer, a, b or c.**

1 *In traditional Indian families the bride and groom used to meet for the first time at*
   a the marriage.
   b the bride's home.
   c the groom's home.

2 *In India the father of the bride used to give*
   a the bride a gift.
   b the groom some money.
   c the groom's family a gift.

3 *Recently it has become popular for Indian families to*
   a use websites to find marriage partners for their children.
   b ask their children to get married online.
   c send their children abroad to find a partner.

4 *In India these days, more and more married couples live*
   a with the bride's family.
   b on their own.
   c with the groom's family.

Practice for the test

Section 3

 Questions 1–2

You will hear two students discussing a project on international festivals with their tutor. Choose the correct letter, a, b or c.

1 *The students are planning to study*

    a different types of celebration.

    b how the festivals started.

    c people's attitudes to festivals.

2 *The students have already discovered*

    a the seasons in different countries.

    b how the Carnival is linked to different times of the year.

    c similarities between countries that are far away from each other.

 Questions 3–5

Now you will hear the next part of the recording. Choose THREE letters, a–g.

What do the students say about the changes in the Carnival since it started?

    a It has turned into a church celebration.

    b It celebrates the end of winter.

    c It is only celebrated in Europe.

    d It is celebrated in many different regions.

    e It takes place during the rainy season.

    f It is not connected with the seasons.

    g It is celebrated when the weather is very hot.

3 what ....

4 where ....

5 when ....

 Questions 6–10

Now listen to the last part of the recording. Write NO MORE THAN THREE WORDS OR A NUMBER for each answer.

6 What else are the students going to research?

....

7 How many countries do they know of where festivals involve water?

....

8 What three meanings can water have? ....

9 What do water festivals celebrate? ....

10 How are the Carnival and the seasons linked?

....

Writing

Develop your exam skills

> **info**
>
> In the Task 2 essay, you may have to justify an opinion, explain causes and effects, or outline problems and suggest solutions. In an opinion essay, you must give your opinions, along with reasons and examples.

1 **Read the essay title and possible topics below. Then choose the topic of the essay, a, b or c, that matches.**

All museums and art galleries should be free because they are an important part of a country's culture.

How far do you agree with this statement?

a   a country's culture

b   the importance of museums and art galleries

c   free entrance to museums and art galleries

2 **Read the essay question in Exercise 1 again and then read the alternative questions below. Choose the question, a, b or c, that has the same meaning.**

a   How far do you agree that museums and art galleries are an important part of a country's culture?

b   How far do you agree that it is a good idea for museums and art galleries to be free for cultural reasons?

c   How far do you agree that museums and art galleries are good?

3 **Read the essay question below. What does it say children *do* and what does it say is the *result*? Which question, a, b or c, matches the essay question?**

Children watch too much television nowadays and this is bad for their education and development.

How far do you agree with this statement?

a   To what extent do you agree that if children watch too much television, they do not learn or develop well?

b   To what extent do you agree that television is bad for children?

c   To what extent do you agree that watching television means that children learn nothing?

4 **Read the four ideas below that either agree or disagree with the statement in the essay question in Exercise 3. Write A (agree) or D (disagree) next to each idea. Which ideas do you agree with?**

1   There are many interesting and educational programmes on television. ....

2   Watching too much television makes children lazy because they do less sport. ....

3   Watching some television is fine but watching too much television is bad for children. ....

4   Many children learn through visual activities, so watching television can help them. ....

Exam tip

Task 2 questions are often a statement followed by one of the following questions:

How far do you agree with this statement? OR *To what extent do you agree with this statement?*

These questions both mean: *To what extent do you agree with the statement?*

see **GRAMMAR** page 159 and get more **PRACTICE** online

5 **Read the essay question and the ideas that follow. Why is the first idea too general? Decide which ideas 2–6 answer the question or just describe the topic in general. Write Q (question) or T (topic) next to each idea.**

All children should learn to play a musical instrument at school. How far do you agree with this statement?

1 Music is fun for children so they enjoy it. ......T......

2 Learning to play a musical instrument is a good idea because it helps children learn useful skills like coordination and self-motivation. ....

3 Learning to play a musical instrument is difficult so not all children can do it. ....

4 Listening to music helps children relax so it is good for their health. ....

5 Schools should include subjects such as music in the timetable because they are creative. ....

6 Learning a musical instrument at school is good but playing sport and other activities are also important for children. ....

6 **Read the essay question below and complete sentences 1–4 with your own ideas. Then write four or five of your own ideas about the same essay topic. Give your reasons and use the conjunctions *and*, *but*, *because* and *so*.**

Countries should not replace their traditional culture with modern culture. To what extent do you agree with this statement?

1 Traditional culture is important because ....

2 Modern culture is important because ....

3 Young people often prefer modern culture but ....

4 Both traditional and modern culture are popular so ....

Practice for the test

Task 2

You should spend about 40 minutes on this task.

Write about the following topic:

Young people should spend more time on cultural activities such as music and theatre and less time on sport.

How far do you agree with this statement?

Give reasons for your answer and include any relevant examples from your own knowledge or experience.

Write at least 175 words.

Unit 4

Places to live

Speaking

pronunciation • syllables and word stress • *there is / there are* • fluency

Develop your exam skills

info

Part 1 of the Speaking test tests your ability to talk about everyday topics.

Part 2 tests your ability to talk about a specific topic and to organize your ideas.

1 **Read the question and answer. What do you think are the good and bad points about the answer?**

A: How would you describe your hometown? B: Busy. Dirty. I don't like it.

2 **Prepare your answer to the question in Exercise 1. Make notes on the ideas below.**

- location of the city, town or village (area? country?) and size (population?)
- positive words to describe a city, town or village
- places tourists visit
- your opinion and an example to support it

3 **Record your answer to the question. Use your notes to help you.**

🎧 29 **4** **Listen to a student's answer to the question in Exercise 1 and assess it. Use the table. Then listen and assess the recording of your own answer.**

	Model answer	Your answer
Is the answer too slow or too fast?		
Are there pauses?		
Are there any grammar errors?		
Are words repeated?		

5 **How can you improve your answer? Record your answer again and try to improve your technique and language.**

Exam tip

Try to give long answers, not just two or three words. Speak at a natural speed, not fast and not slow, and without lots of pauses. Use synonyms and a good range of vocabulary. Practise your grammar to help you use the correct forms.

In Part 2 of the
Speaking test, use
the one minute
to think and plan.
Identify the topic on
the card. Make notes
on the three points
and the summary
point. This organizes
your answer. Think
of suitable topic
vocabulary and
grammar structures.
Then speak at a
natural speed for two
minutes.

see **GRAMMAR**
page 142 and get
more **PRACTICE** online

6 Read the Part 2 task card and the candidate's notes. Which notes are not useful? Why?

> **Describe an area of your country you know and like.**
>
> You should say:
>
> where it is
> what its special features are
> what you and other people do in this area
>
> and explain why you like it.

name of city (English translation?)
description of country
It's near ...
It's got ... / There's ...
tourists — try food, take photos
me — relax, meet friends, play sports
other cities I like
my opinion and example

7 Prepare your answer to the Part 2 task in Exercise 6. You have one minute to make notes. Use the Exam tip box to help you.

8 Look at your notes again. Can you improve them? Now record your answer. You have two minutes to give your answer.

Practice for the test

Part 1

1 Read the Part 1 questions. Then listen and match the answers a–g to the questions.

1 Do you work or are you a student? ....
2 What do you like about your job? / What do you like about studying? ....
3 When do you see your friends and family? ....
4 Where is your hometown located? ....
5 What do people in your town do? ....
6 Is it easy to travel around your hometown? ....
7 Is there a good health system where you live? ....

2 Record your answers to the questions in Exercise 1.

Part 2

3 Read the instructions for the Part 2 task card. You have one minute to make notes for your answer.

> **Describe an interesting city you know and like.**
>
> You should say:
>
> where it is
> how you went there
> what you did there
>
> and explain why you found it so interesting.

4 Now record your answer to the task in Exercise 3. You have two minutes to give your answer.

Comparing and contrasting charts and graphs for Task 1

Develop your exam skills

info

For Task 1 you may have to describe and compare two or more charts, graphs or tables. These may show information about the same topic but focus on different aspects.

You will need to understand what information each chart / graph / table shows and find the relationships between them. For example, you may need to notice a change in one table / chart / graph that could be caused or be the cause of a change in another table / chart / graph.

see GRAMMAR page 144 and get more PRACTICE online

1 **Look at the bar chart and the two pie charts. Talk with your partner about what each chart shows. Then complete the sentences.**

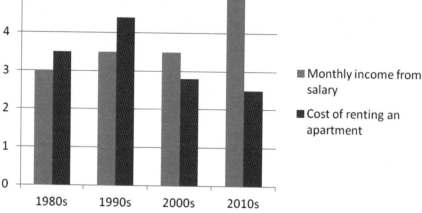

Average income and accommodation costs (in hundred $) per person in Toronto

■ Monthly income from salary

■ Cost of renting an apartment

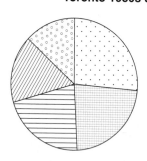

Toronto 1980s & 1990s

- ⊡ Entertainment
- ▤ Sport
- ▤ Food and clothing
- ▨ Home improvements
- ▨ Gas & Electricity

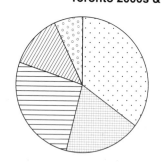

Toronto 2000s & 2010s

- ⊡ Entertainment
- ▤ Sport
- ▤ Food and clothing
- ▨ Home improvements
- ▨ Gas & Electricity

1 During the 2000s and 2010s people in Toronto spent more on entertainment because they *had higher salaries* .

2 Due to higher monthly salaries people spent more on food and clothing in the ....

3 Spending on entertainment was .... in the 1990s because the cost of renting an apartment was high.

4 People spent more on sport and entertainment in the 2000s because it was
.... to rent an apartment.

5 In the 1990s the .... was the highest so people spent
less on other things.

6 In the 2010s monthly salaries were high and rent costs were low so people spent
more on .... than in the 1990s.

Exam tip

It is important to find
and explain the **main
trends** shown by the
graph(s) / chart(s). Do
not describe all the
details in the graph(s) /
chart(s). Look at these
example sentences
describing the charts
in Exercise 1:

*The cost of renting
an apartment was
low in the 2000s so
people spent more
on other things.* =
MAIN TREND

*Spending on gas and
electricity in Toronto
was higher in the
1980s than in the
2000s.* = DETAIL

2 **Read the sentences and decide which are the main trends and which are
details, according to the charts in Exercise 1. Write M (main trends) or D
(details).**

1 The money spent on home improvements was less in the 2000s and 2010s.
....D....

2 Spending on leisure activities grew over this period. ....

3 Monthly incomes in Toronto increased from the 1980s to the 2010s. ....

4 The cost of renting an apartment has decreased since the 1980s. ....

5 People have spent more on entertainment and sport in recent years. ....

6 From the 1980s to the 1990s monthly salaries and the cost of renting an
apartment increased. ....

7 In the 2010s people's spending on entertainment was higher. ....

3 **Look at the graph and the bar chart and write T (True) or F (False) next to
each sentence 1–6.**

1 Land used for housing has decreased since 1980. ....T....

2 The city of Newtown has expanded the area of its park land over the last
30 years. ....

3 The cost of all land types increased in 2010. ....

4 In 2000 more land was used for housing than for offices and shops. ....

5 The price of business land was the highest in 1980. ....

6 The amount of land used for business purposes grew from 2000 to 2010. ....

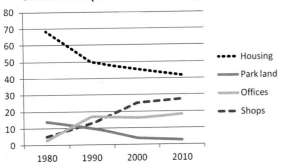

**Land use (per km²) within the city limits
of Newtown (total area = 90km²)**

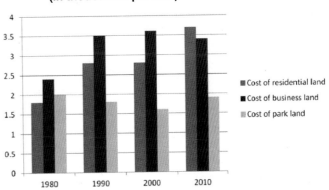

**Average cost of land in Newtown
(in thousand £ per km²)**

4 **Expand these notes into full sentences to describe the graph and bar chart in Exercise 3. Study the example answer carefully before doing 2–6.**

1 cost of residential land = increase / land use for housing = decrease / since 1980

Since 1980 the cost of residential land has increased so the land used for housing has decreased.

2 1990 to 2000 / business land cost = slight rise / land used for shops and offices = same

3 since 2000 / cost of business land and business land use = stable

4 housing land use / decrease / last 40 years / reason = cost

5 land used for offices / from 1980 to 2000 / grew

6 cheapest land = park land / 1980–2010

Practice for the test

Task 1

You should spend about 20 minutes on this task.

The pie charts and the table show the types of living accommodation occupied by 25-year-olds in London during the 1990s and the 2010s, and the availability of different types of accommodation in London during the same two periods.

Summarize the information by selecting and reporting the main features and make comparisons where relevant.

Write at least 150 words.

Survey of 25-year-olds' accommodation in London - 1990s

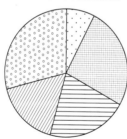

Survey of 25-year-olds' accommodation in London - 2010s

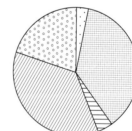

- ⬚ House (alone)
- ⬚ House (shared)
- ⬚ Flat (alone)
- ⬚ Flat (shared)
- ⬚ With parents

Available housing in London: 1990s – 2010s: 1990s and 2010 onwards				
	1–2 bedroom houses	1–2 bedroom flats	3–4 bedroom houses	3–4 bedroom flats
1990s	34,000	32,000	47,000	39,000
2010 onwards	12,000	10,000	48,500	32,000

Reading

Matching features

Get READY for class!
Remember to do your preparation before class.
online • workbook

Develop your exam skills

info

In the exam, you may be asked to match a list of factual statements or opinions to a group of features taken from a text. The information in the list of statements will not be in the same order as the information in the text.

1 The words below can be organized in three groups; two groups are grammatical and one relates to meaning. What are the three groups? Complete the table with the three categories and examples from the box.

Category 1:	Category 2:	Category 3:
organization	he	educational

organization he educational
community communal team
her cast practical crowd they
loyal band academic she theirs
criminal them safe mine party

2 Look at paragraph A of the newsletter on page 42. Think about how the phrase *fundraising event* describes what the paragraph is about. Write one or two words from each paragraph B–G that describe them.

A fundraising event (walk)

B ....

C ....

D ....

E ....

F ....

G ....

3 Read the text again. How many of the paragraphs mention the following? Write the letters A–G.

1 money ....

2 dogs ....

3 problems in the community ....

4 activities for children ....

5 activities that involve food ....

6 people who live(d) locally ....

7 volunteers ....

4 Read the statements below. Then find and underline paraphrases in the text. The statements are in the same order as the paraphrases in the text.

1 We have just planted many new trees.

2 There will be another group meeting so that everyone can practise before the real interviews.

3 Many people turned up to the Forest Schools activities.

4 You need to enrol before you can attend any of these activities.

5 The winner will receive a big chocolate egg.

6 Because many people have been asking for it, …

Warley Woods Community Trust

Welcome to our third newsletter of the year!

A   Our main activity for March is our *Walk for the Woods* fundraising event on Saturday, 17th March, starting any time between 10 a.m. and 2 p.m. In recognition of locally born Jack Judge, who wrote the song 'It's a long way to Tipperary' 100 years ago, we will be walking the distance between Warley Woods and Tipperary. It is indeed a long way – 260 miles – so we need a lot of people to do a lot of one-mile laps round the Woods. The more people that you can get to sponsor you, the more money we can raise to help look after our beautiful woodland. Sponsor forms are available from the shop at the Woods or on our website.

B   Lots of new trees have gone in recently. The Sunday volunteers planted two beeches and an oak in the meadow last week. This was thanks to a grant from the Big Tree Plant and to Lisa and Gordon Whitaker, whose friends gave money for the big trees instead of wedding presents. Thanks to everyone who took part, including Lisa and Gordon and South Staffordshire plc, who dug the big holes for us. (There is a DVD of one of the volunteers falling in – or was he pushed?)

C   There were 15 volunteers at the Oral History Training Day, which was led very ably by Julia Letts. Lots of issues were discussed and ideas considered. The group will be meeting again and will have the opportunity to do some practice interviews before starting to interview the local people who have offered to tell their stories. We are happy to hear from any others who would like to be interviewed about their memories of the Woods for the project. If you or anyone you know is interested, please contact Viv Cole at the office. This project is funded by Heritage Lottery Fund.

D   We already have sponsors for two of our events this year. Derek Spires, a local estate agent, is sponsoring *Theatre in the Woods,* which this year is a performance of *Much Ado About Nothing,* and will take place on Thursday, 14th June. Also, Companion Care Vets are sponsoring the picnic. We are still looking for a sponsor for the *All about Dogs* event on 9th September, so if you or any company you know would like to do this, please get in touch with the office.

E   The trustees have been giving some thought to ways of minimizing future damage to the fountain and have decided to contact a specialist local firm to see what can be done about the graffiti.

F   There was a huge response to the Forest Schools activities held at half term. These will be held again during the Easter holidays on the following dates: 4th, 5th and 11th April from 10 a.m. to 3 p.m. for children over eight. On 12th April, from 10 a.m. to 12 noon, there will be a Teddy Bears' Picnic for the under eights. All sessions must be booked in advance and forms are available at the shop or office.

G   Finally, don't forget the Easter Egg Roll on Bank Holiday Monday, 9th April, starting at 11 a.m. Bring your £1.00 entry money and your own hard-boiled and decorated egg to roll down the hill in the woods. The first past the finishing line will win a massive chocolate egg! This year, due to popular demand, there will also be an Adults' Easter Egg Roll following the children's competition.

We look forward to seeing you all soon at one of our many events!

Glossary

trust: a group of people or an organization that has control of an amount of money or property and invests it on behalf of other people or as a charity • *trustee:* someone with legal control of money or property that is kept or invested for another person, company or organization

Questions 1–9

**Read the text. Then match each sentence 1–9 with the correct group A–D.
You can use any letter more than once.**

1 People feel safe here. ....

2 These exist in different forms. ....

3 People support each other. ....

4 It is difficult to say exactly what they are. ....

5 They have a lot to offer their members. ....

6 People can do things on a bigger scale. ....

7 The members meet up in person. ....

8 People are prepared to take on other people's responsibilities. ....

9 People are strangers. ....

This is true for:

A all communities

B online communities

C traditional communities

D none of the mentioned communities

The importance of community

A community is not easy to define. In this essay, I will examine what transforms individuals into a community and discuss some different types. I will also look at what all communities have in common, the benefits they offer and draw conclusions about their increasing importance.

The word 'community' may trigger images of traditional communities in the developing world, where large families live together. Elderly parents live with their children and grandchildren in one house. Parents have relative freedom: for example, if they leave the house, there is always someone left behind to look after their children. We may also imagine the neighbours as people who are happy to help out whenever it is needed. The stereotypical view is that of a village, where people have little but can feel very rich.

At the other end of the spectrum, there are ultramodern communities, where the members are unlikely to have met each other. These are online communities, where people blog or chat about issues that are important to them. They come across others on websites and may develop a relationship with like-minded people. The view is often that these are artificial bonds between people who are still isolated strangers.

In reality, this is not true as the connections are real. Moreover, there are many types of communities in between these extremes: for example, people who join sports and leisure clubs, who sign up with voluntary, political, religious or other organizations, or who take part in group discussions in their local area. They may be campaigning about issues or simply getting together for companionship and support.

Human beings are social by nature, so it should not be a surprise that we organize ourselves in groups. However, there is more going on: these groups provide something that we cannot achieve on our own. The main benefit of being part of a larger group is strength in numbers. For example, we can access and share more information, we can take part in team sports, we can complain and campaign more effectively and feel supported in whatever we do.

The stereotypical views of the happy village and the isolated computer users may not be completely true, but what we do know is that what defines them is the sense of identity and security that they provide for their members: the knowledge that there are people who we have something in common with and who can be relied on to be there when we need each other.

Listening

labelling maps and flow charts • answering short-answer questions • completing sentences

Get READY for class!

Remember to do your preparation before class.

online • workbook

Develop your exam skills

> **info**
>
> In the exam you may have to complete some sentences. You will use the exact words you hear in the recording, but it is important to make sure your answers are grammatically correct. You will lose points if they are not.

1 Complete the sentences with the words below.

> the corner   the right   to the lake   straight ahead of you   opposite   Medical Centre

1 Take the lift up to the twelfth floor; the tutor's office is the third door on ....

2 To get to the bank, cross the road at the library and turn left at ....

3 Go down the footpath to the main road and the station's right ....

4 Turn left at the top of the stairs, go along to the end of the corridor and you'll see the seminar room ....

5 Take the second road on the right, then first left, and you'll find the physics building next to the ....

6 Go along the main path as far as the canteen and then follow it round to the left until you get ....

2 🎧 31 You will hear six short conversations where one person is explaining to another how to find different places on campus. Think about some of the expressions you expect to hear. Then listen and complete the sentences. Write NO MORE THAN THREE WORDS in each sentence. Pay attention to your spelling and grammar.

1 The Sports Centre is on the other side ....

2 The lecture theatre in the Law School is on ....

3 To reach the Business School, you take the footpath ....

4 The theatre is ....

5 The nearest bus stop is opposite the ....

6 The bank is .... to the shop.

> **info**
>
> In another type of question you may be asked to answer questions using short answers. You will hear the words you should use on the recording. You do not need to change them but it is very important to pay attention to the number of words you write. You will be told how many words to use. This is usually no more than three words and/or a number. Your answer will be marked incorrect if you use too many words.

3 🎧 32 You will hear Sandra and Tom talking about the facilities on campus. Listen and answer the questions. Write NO MORE THAN TWO WORDS.

1 Which floor is the library coffee shop on? ....

2 What does Sandra like to do there? ....

3 Where is the silent zone? ....

4 Where does Tom live? ....

5 How many people live in Sandra's house? ....

6 What does Tom often do near Sandra's house? ....

4 You will hear two students talking about the different food outlets on a university campus. Label the plan below.

A Fast food hall   D College dining room

B Snack bar   E Italian restaurant

C Mexican restaurant

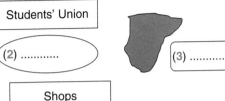

Practice for the test

Section 1

 Questions 1–4

You will hear Lily explaining to Chen how to use the library. Label the plan of the library.

A PC Zone   B Library café   C Cookbooks   D Travel   E Silent zone

Ground floor   First floor

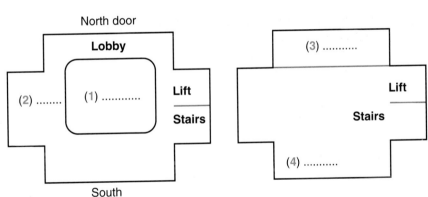

 Questions 5–7

Now listen to the next part of the recording and complete the sentences. Write **NO MORE THAN TWO WORDS**.

5 First look up the title in the ....

6 The class mark is one or two letters and ....

7 The .... shows you where to look for the books.

 Questions 8–10

Now listen to the last part of the recording and answer the questions. Write **NO MORE THAN THREE WORDS**.

8 What do you need to scan first? ....

9 What does the scanner do when you scan a book? ....

10 What does the system do at the end? ....

Unit 5

Arts and media

Writing

Analysing and describing a pie chart

Develop your exam skills

Get READY for class!
Remember to do your preparation before class.
online • workbook

> **info**
>
> A pie chart is a circle (or 'pie') divided into sections. The whole circle represents the total quantity (100%) and the sections show how the total is divided into different shares or proportions. These shares or proportions correspond to different categories. Pie charts are useful for comparing these categories. Proportions are shown as a percentage (%) or fraction (e.g. ½) of the total quantity.

1 **Look at the pie charts A and B about DVD sales. Match sentences 1–6 to the pie charts. Write A or B next to each sentence.**

A **UK DVD sales by film genre 2009**   B **UK DVD sales by film genre 2009**

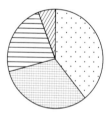

☐ Comedy
▦ Thriller
▤ Horror
▨ Documentary

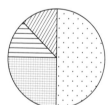

☐ Comedy
▦ Thriller
▤ Horror
▨ Documentary

1 Fifty per cent of the DVDs sold in 2009 were comedy films. ....B....

2 A third of DVD sales were comedy films. ....

3 Thrillers were 25 per cent of the total UK DVD sales in 2009. ....

4 Horror films were about a quarter of DVD sales in the UK in 2009. ....

5 In 2009 comedy films were half the total DVD sales in the UK. ....

6 Less than 10 per cent of DVDs sold in the UK in 2009 were documentary films. ....

see GRAMMAR page 151 and get more PRACTICE online

2 Look at the pie chart about visits to the cinema. Write sentences describing the chart using the words and phrases from the box.

Cinema visitors by age group

approximately   just over   just under   almost   nearly

Example: *Approximately 10 per cent of cinema visitors are between 40 and 54 years old.*

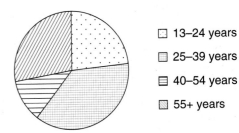

☐ 13–24 years
☐ 25–39 years
☐ 40–54 years
☐ 55+ years

info

In Task 1 there are sometimes two or three pie charts that you must compare. The pie charts may represent different years and show trends over time. You need to describe the changes and similarities and / or differences between the pie charts.

3 Look at the pie charts about ways of watching films. Decide if the sentences are T (true) or F (false). Then correct the false sentences.

Formats for watching films 1992   **Formats for watching films 2008**

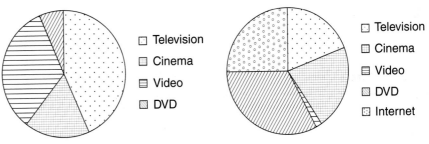

☐ Television
☐ Cinema
☐ Video
☐ DVD

☐ Television
☐ Cinema
☐ Video
☐ DVD
☐ Internet

1   The pie charts show how many people watched films in 1992 and 2008.
........................*F*..................

2   The pie charts show the proportion of films watched on different formats in 1992 and 2008. ....

3   More people watched films on television in 2008 than in 1992. ....

4   In 1992 nearly a third of films were watched on video but this amount decreased to about two per cent in 2008. ....

5   The proportion of people watching films at the cinema was about the same in 1992 and 2008. ....

6   There was a slight increase in the number of people watching films on DVD from 1992 to 2008. ....

7   In 1992 no one used the Internet to watch films but in 2008 people used the Internet to watch a quarter of all films. ....

8   In 2008 approximately half of the films were watched using two formats: the cinema and the Internet. ....

9   From 1992 to 2008 the number of people watching films on television decreased by just over 25 per cent. ....

10   From 1992 to 2008 the number of people watching films on television decreased to approximately half. ....

see **GRAMMAR** page 152 and more **PRACTICE** online

4 **Look at the pie charts showing reasons for buying films. Complete the text about the charts.**

Reasons for buying films – Men

☐ Soundtrack
☐ Story
☐ Special effects
☐ Genre
☐ Actors
☐ Cost

Reasons for buying films – Women

☐ Soundtrack
☐ Story
☐ Special effects
☐ Genre
☐ Actors
☐ Cost

The pie charts show the different reasons why (**1**) _men and women_ buy films. In general, most people buy films because of the (**2**) .... and the actors. The (**3**) .... is the least important reason why people buy films.

We can see from the pie chart that almost (**4**) .... of men choose films because of the special effects. Another important reason for men is the music; (**5**) .... 20 per cent of men buy a film for its soundtrack. The reasons for women are different. (**6**) .... of women buy films for the story and the actors; the other reasons are much less important. Special effects are the least important reason for women; only about (**7**) .... of women are interested in them. The (**8**) .... of men and women who choose films based on the cost is (**9**) .... the same, at about ten (**10**) ....

Practice for the test

Task 1

You should spend about 20 minutes on this task.

The pie charts below show the share of Oscar winners by film genre for 2003 and 2008. Summarize the information by selecting and reporting the main features, and make comparisons where relevant.

Write at least 150 words.

Oscar winners in 2003 by genre

☐ Thriller
☐ Documentary
☐ Romance
☐ Science Fiction
☐ Action
☐ Comedy
☐ Horror

Oscar winners in 2008 by genre

☐ Thriller
☐ Documentary
☐ Romance
☐ Science Fiction
☐ Action
☐ Comedy
☐ Horror

Reading

Completing sentences

Develop your exam skills

ℹ️ In the exam, you may be asked to complete sentences with words from the passage. The information will be in the same order as the questions.

1 Try to match the words with their (near) synonyms. Then look up the words in a dictionary.

1	device	**a**	difficult choice
2	dilemma	**b**	truth
3	fiction	**c**	the future
4	magazines and books	**d**	gadget
5	tomorrow	**e**	curiosity
6	fact	**f**	story
7	interest	**g**	reading material

2 Try to match the words with their (near) antonyms. Then look up the words in a dictionary.

1	digital	**a**	the future
2	yesterday	**b**	deliberate
3	rise	**c**	reality
4	fiction	**d**	analogue
5	lost	**e**	decline
6	accidental	**f**	found

3 Read the sentences and underline the words or phrases that refer to similar ideas or things. The first one has been done for you.

1 E-books, or <u>books that are read on a digital device</u> rather than as a print book, are growing in popularity.

2 These types of books can be read on a variety of computers or on e-readers, mobile electronic devices that are made especially for reading books.

3 E-readers are light and easy to carry, and that is just one of their advantages.

4 There was a decline in sales of e-readers a few years ago, but this fall lasted only for a short while.

5 Many e-readers include software which lets readers buy and borrow e-books from libraries and shops directly; they don't have to waste time downloading them onto a computer first.

4 Scan the text on page 50 to find the following words or their (near) synonyms. Try to find as many as you can in less than 90 seconds. They are in the same order.

1	enjoy	6	stopping	11	useful
2	full of	7	small	12	unknown
3	re-read	8	outweigh	13	worsens
4	assemble	9	mobile	14	larger
5	interest	10	permits	15	odd

Are e-books the future?

Those of us who delight in reading will know the problem: our book shelves are crammed with old favourites, books we plan to re-read, and books we have not quite started yet. We collect stories that have caught our interest and find it hard to let them go. There is another way though: e-readers allow us to hold all our much-loved works of fiction in one hand. So what is preventing us from replacing our bookcases with one compact digital device, an e-reader?

The advantages of e-readers certainly seem to outweigh the disadvantages. They are light and mobile devices that can be taken anywhere. Taking one gadget on holiday allows us to take hundreds of novels with us without having to pay for extra luggage on the plane.

The electronic nature of e-readers gives us so much more than a print copy of a book can do. It lets us read in the dark (handy in case of a power cut). We can look up unfamiliar words in the in-built dictionary with just one click, we can make notes, and we never forget what page we were on: the e-reader remembers that for us. If our eyesight declines, we can make the letters bigger. We can re-read Jane Eyre as often as we like and the book will never look any worse for it. And even if our taste in books is odd, nobody need know: others

can't see what we are reading. Not only that, most e-books are cheaper than their print versions, and many older books can be downloaded for free.

So why have only one in three of us read an e-book? The answer must be that there is something special about the look, the feel, and maybe even the smell of printed books. 'Real' books are objects that have a past and their physical presence surrounds us with happy memories.

Practice for the test

Questions 1–5

Complete the sentences below. Choose NO MORE THAN TWO WORDS OR NUMBERS from the text for each answer.

1 Scientists have already found out a lot about our minds but they are not sure yet about all their ....

2 Our brains need to work hard while we are read, so reading is definitely not something ....

3 In order to solve problems, you need to use your ....

4 Readers learn to think and write better so reading can help a person prepare for ....

5 Education is about learning more and increasing ....

How literature is good for us

Reading fiction is considered by many people to be a waste of time. After all, reading stories is not a creative activity, nor does it seem educational. Surely we can't learn anything useful from made-up stories?

Science, however, would disagree. Just like games and puzzles can keep our brains active, so does reading. By using our brains, it is possible to slow down age-related mental deterioration. Recent research also suggests that a good story can change our brain structure, both in the short term and in the longer term: reading about the actions and feelings of a character in a book seems to trick our brains into believing we have experienced them ourselves. However, behavioural research still needs to be carried out to confirm these scientific findings.

While we wait for science to confirm the benefits of reading, keen readers do not need to be convinced. They know reading is good for you. When we read, we have to take in a lot of information about the characters and their stories, and we have to remember these details in order to want to keep reading. The more we read, therefore, the more we exercise our memories.

Reading is not a passive activity: we increase our vocabulary by repeatedly being exposed to certain words, we use our critical thinking skills to decide if the story makes sense, and when we read mysteries or detective stories, we use our analytical skills to try to work out the solutions to the mysteries or crimes.

Reading and writing are also closely interlinked, and the more we read a variety of styles, the more likely it is that our own writing will improve. Looking at it this way, it does seem that reading literature is good training for higher education.

We also build knowledge when we read: we can have a virtual experience of the cultures of countries we have never visited and we can learn about the customs of the past: the fashions, the food, pastimes and other aspects of life. And even when the stories are rooted in the here and now, we can find out more about topics that we may not come across in our daily lives, for example, about the lives of people from different social or educational backgrounds or the attitudes of those with different interests to ours. Stories add to our understanding and knowledge of the world, so they appear to be educational after all.

Last but not least, reading lets us escape into another time and place – into another world. Admittedly, reading is not a creative activity, but why should we always have to produce something? In the real world, where people work hard and life can be challenging, isn't it wonderful that we can find relief in a fictional world and forget our own troubles for a little? This escape surely helps us to cope better with our own lives.

Speaking

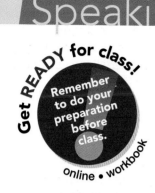

Get READY for class!
Remember to do your preparation before class.
online • workbook

Develop your exam skills

info Part 2 tests your ability to talk without pausing and also your ability to plan and organize your answer.

1 Read the Part 2 task card below. Look at the underlined key words. Then match the key words with the notes a student made. There is one extra note.

> **Talk about a programme you learnt something from.**
>
> You should say:
>
> what <u>type of programme</u> it was
> which your <u>favourite parts</u> were
> <u>who</u> you watched it with
>
> and <u>explain what</u> you learnt from it.

1 interesting interviews with the writer's family and friends

2 learnt about the writer's life, e.g. poor family, no qualifications, lived in different countries, now lives in her hometown

3 documentary about a writer

4 watched it at college

5 with my classmates

2 Read a student's answer to the task in Exercise 1. Assess it and write T (true) or F (false) next to each sentence 1–3.

> I'd like to talk about a programme I learnt something from. It was about a writer and I learnt about the writer's life. She was from a poor family and I learnt she had no qualifications from school. After leaving school, she lived in different countries. I learnt that she now lives in her hometown and she writes there. I watched it with my classmates. We watched it at college in a seminar. Then we talked about her life. It was a documentary about this famous writer. I always enjoy reading her books. She writes about college students and their lives.

1 All the key words and notes are included. ....

2 The answer follows the order on the task card. ....

3 The answer is clear and easy to follow. ....

Exam tip

Follow the order of the points on the task card. These organize your answer and help you to keep talking.

3 Read another student's answer to the task in Exercise 1. Assess it and write T (true) or F (false) next to each sentence 1–3.

> I'd like to talk about a programme I learnt something from. The programme was a very interesting documentary and it was about a famous writer. I often watch this documentary series because it always has really interesting people or topics.
>
> Firstly, I liked everything in the documentary but my favourite parts were the interviews with her family and friends. A good example of this is the interview with her sister. She talked about their life when they were young children. She was very funny. There was also one old friend from the writer's school; they are still friends and they usually meet up every year. I liked learning about the writer's personal life.

I watched the programme with my classmates at college in a seminar. It was part of the course, and then we gave a presentation about her life. I learnt lots of things from the documentary, for example, the writer was from a poor family, she had no qualifications and she lived in different countries. Finally, I learnt that she now lives in her hometown and never goes abroad these days.

1 All the key words and notes are included. ....

2 The answer follows the order on the task card. ....

3 The answer is clear and easy to follow. ....

see **GRAMMAR** page 143 and more **PRACTICE** online

4 **Read the student's answer in Exercise 3 again. Find and <u>underline</u> two words or phrases for giving examples. Then find two words or phrases for organizing the answer.**

see **GRAMMAR** page 157 and more **PRACTICE** online

5 **Plan your own Part 2 answer using the task card in Exercise 1.**

- Make notes on each key word.
- Write sentences using your notes.
- Include the underlined phrases from Exercise 3.

6 **Record your answer using your notes to help. Then listen to your answer to see if you can improve it. Answer again, but refer only to the task card in Exercise 1, not your notes.**

Practice for the test

Part 1

1 **Read the Part 1 questions. Record your answer to each question.**

When did you last watch television?

What do you usually watch on television?

What are some popular programmes in your country?

Why do you think some TV programmes are popular?

Part 2

2 **Read the Part 2 task card. Plan your answer. You have one minute for this in the exam. Then record your answer. You have one to two minutes for this in the exam.**

> **Talk about a TV programme you enjoy watching.**
>
> You should say:
>
> what type of programme it is
> which your favourite parts are
> when and where you watch it
>
> and explain why you enjoy watching it.

Exam tip

Remember that there are different topics and different task cards in each IELTS exam. Do not memorize a speech on a topic for the exam.

Get READY for class!

Remember to do your preparation before class.

online • workbook

Exam tip

When you are looking at the key words in the questions before listening, do not forget to include the question words. These will tell you what kind of information you need (e.g. *What type of ...* = category, class).

Develop your exam skills

info

In this type of question you have to complete a table with words or a number. Remember to keep to the word count. Also remember that the heading will tell you what kind of information you need to focus on. Before you listen, it may be helpful to underline the heading of each column in the table.

1 **Read the questions. Underline the key words and the question words. Then predict answers to the questions.**

1 What is the most common crime in the UK? ....

2 What two forms of theft does the police officer mention? ....

3 Why are people in more danger when they are abroad? ....

4 What should people leave in the hotel when they are on holiday? ....

5 What kind of mobile is popular with thieves? ....

37 **2** **You will hear an extract from a radio programme with information about crime in the UK. Answer the questions in Exercise 1. Write NO MORE THAN FOUR WORDS.**

38 **3** **You will hear a talk about emergency phone numbers in different countries. Complete the table.**

UK	USA	Australia	Germany	India
999				

4 **Read what a campus security officer says about staying safe on campus. Then read the question and tick the correct letter, a, b or c.**

> Our campus is generally a very safe place for students and staff. Crime is very rare but when it does occur, it's quite often because someone has not been careful enough. They may not have locked their door or they might have gone out alone at night.

What does the security officer say about crime on campus?

a The campus is always safe.

b Crime does not happen very often.

c Crime never happens when people are careful.

see **GRAMMAR**
page 143 and more
PRACTICE online

5 **Study the explanations below and compare them with your own answer. Notice that the difference between the correct answer and a wrong answer may depend on one word.**

> a The campus is always safe: he says the *campus is generally a very safe place*, not that it is <u>always</u> safe.
>
> b Crime does not happen very often: he says crime is *very rare,* meaning *it does not happen very often*.
>
> c Crime never happens when people are careful: he says crime *often* happens when *someone has not been careful enough,* not that it <u>never</u> happens when people are careful.

39 **6** You will hear a campus talk about staying safe at university. Discuss the questions and predict the answers. Then listen and choose the correct letter.

1 *When can students ask a security officer to walk home with them?*

    a in the evening   **b** after dark   **c** late at night

2 *What does the security officer say students should do if they want to go home late at night and they feel nervous?*

    a ring campus security   **b** study in the library   **c** go home alone

3 *What does the he say about national and on-campus emergency numbers?*

    a They are both 999.   **b** They are both 3333.   **c** They are not the same.

4 *Why should students call 3333 in an emergency on campus?*

    a 999 does not work.   **b** It is confusing.   **c** It is faster.

Practice for the test

Section 2

40 **Questions 1–4**

You will hear a talk about safety in different regions. Complete the table about crime in two holiday destinations. Write **NO MORE THAN TWO WORDS OR A NUMBER.**

Region	Type of crime
(1)	(2) ....
(3)	(4) ....

41 **Questions 5–7**

Now you will hear the next part of the recording. Listen and answer the questions. Write **NO MORE THAN THREE WORDS** for each answer.

5 What are tourists advised not to wear in the street? ....

6 Where should tourists not go after dark? ....

7 In some parts of Latin America, where do thieves often take money from tourists?
....

42 **Questions 8–10**

Now listen to the last part of the recording. Choose the correct letter, a, b or c.

8 *What did the travel advisor think about India?*

    a It was dangerous.   **b** It was organized.   **c** It was safe.

9 *Why does the speaker recommend going to India with a tour group?*

    a It is more fun.   **b** It is less risky.   **c** They do not need cash.

10 *What did the tour guide tell the tourists not to do?*

    a use their language   **b** go with strangers   **c** be nice and friendly

Unit 6

The natural world

Get READY for class!

Remember to do your preparation before class.

online • workbook

Develop your exam skills

info

Part 1 tests your ability to understand general questions and to give relevant answers. It also tests your ability to expand your answers.

Part 2 tests your ability to talk and develop your ideas about a topic using relevant vocabulary and grammar. It also tests your ability to give a fluent and organized answer.

43 **1** **Read the Part 1 questions and student answers below. Choose the correct answer, a or b. Then listen and check.**

1 How many seasons does your country have?

  a My country has four seasons.

  b There are many seasons in my country.

2 What's your favourite season of the year?

  a Hot and sunny. This is my favourite weather.

  b Summer. This is my favourite season.

3 How do rainy days make you feel?

  a I feel very sad on rainy days.

  b Yes, rainy days make you feel sad.

4 What do you like doing when it's hot?

  a I like it when it's hot, yes.

  b I like going to the beach.

Exam tip

Listen carefully to the question and give a relevant answer. Then expand your answer, for example give a reason or an explanation.

2 **Read the correct answers in Exercise 1 again. Can you make the answers longer? Add a sentence to each correct answer in Exercise 1.**

1 I like it because the weather is hot and sunny.

2 The seasons are spring, summer, autumn and winter.

3 You can go swimming or you can meet friends there.

4 You can't go outside and do any sports.

see **GRAMMAR** page 157 and more **PRACTICE** online

3 **Answer each question in Exercise 1. Include a reason or an explanation in each answer.**

4 Read the task card and the example answer, ignoring the gaps. What is the problem with the example answer? Choose 1 or 2.

1 It includes lots of extra information.

2 It doesn't include extra information.

> **Describe your favourite type of weather.**
>
> You should say:
>
> what the type of weather is
>
> how often you experience this type of weather
>
> what you like doing in this weather
>
> and explain why it is your favourite type of weather.

> I'd like to describe my favourite type of weather. My country has three seasons and there are lots of types of weather. (**1**) .... Yes, wet weather is my favourite. I like going shopping when the weather is wet because the shops are all indoors. (**2**) .... I often experience this weather in other countries. I like travelling in Europe and I always take my umbrella with me. The wet weather lasts for a long time there. (**3**) .... This weather is good for relaxing. For example, you can stay at home and just watch television. (**4**) ....

5 Read sentences a–d. (They all add extra information to the example answer.) Read the answer in Exercise 4 again. Then write the number where each sentence, a–d, goes in the answer.

a It's different from my country as the rainy season only lasts for two months. ....

b You can chat to your friends online too. ....

c I also like cooking delicious meals for my family when there's lots of rain. ....

d It's a difficult choice for me, but I think my favourite is wet weather. ....

6 Add two more sentences to expand any two paragraphs of the example answer in Exercise 3. Then practise giving the answer with a partner.

7 Read the task card in Exercise 3 again. Plan your own answer. Remember to add extra information to each part of your answer.

8 Record your answer. Then listen to a partner's recording and discuss how they could improve it.

Practice for the test

Part 1

Read the Part 1 questions. Record your answer to each question.

1 How many seasons does your country have?

2 What's the weather like in your country?

3 How do rainy days make you feel?

4 What do you like doing when it's hot?

Part 2

Read the Part 2 task card. Plan your answer. You have one minute for this in the exam. Then record your answer. You have one to two minutes for this in the exam.

> **Exam tip**
>
> You can also use vocabulary for free time activities when you talk about the weather. See the activities in your Workbook or Online.

> **Describe your favourite season in your country.**
>
> You should say:
>
> when the season begins and ends
>
> what the weather is like
>
> how it is different from other seasons in your country
>
> and explain why it is your favourite season.

Get READY for class!

Remember to do your preparation before class.

online • workbook

Exam tip

When you do not know the meaning of a word, try to guess by listening for:

- the structure of the word: Is it a noun (e.g. ending in *-ion*, *-ship*, *-ment*, *-er*, *-ist*), an adjective (e.g. ending in *-able*, *-ful*, *-ive*) or a verb (past or present tense)?

- the words that come before and after, e.g. an article, an adjective, etc.

- the context or meaning of the words that surround the word.

- words that sound similar, e.g. *horticulture* sounds a little like *agriculture* and might make you think about *growing* or *farming*.

Develop your exam skills

1 Look at this example and read the explanation. Then read sentences 1–4 carefully and guess the meaning of the <u>underlined</u> words. Think about what helped you guess the meaning.

The <u>bathysphere</u> allowed scientists to explore deeper areas of the ocean bed.

We know that 'bathysphere' is a noun because it has 'the' in front of it, and is followed by a verb. We can guess that it is a piece of equipment because it helped scientists to study the sea bed and we can guess that it is no longer in use because the verb 'allowed' is in the past tense.

1 New <u>submarine</u> technologies are opening up the sea bed for exploration.

2 Fixed oil rigs can only be built in <u>shallow</u> water because they rest on the sea bed.

3 <u>Aquaculture</u> has developed significantly over the last 50 years and now provides 40% of the world's fish.

4 A historic <u>descent</u> to the ocean floor has <u>revealed</u> the existence of mysterious marine creatures that look like huge prawns.

2 Read the sentences in Exercise 1 again. Put the <u>underlined</u> words into the correct column according to their use.

Noun	Adjective	Verb

info When you are asked to label a visual such as a diagram, map or a set of pictures, or complete a flow chart, you may have to select the correct answers from a list of options or you may have to select words from the recording and keep to a specified word limit.

3 🎧 44 You will hear a talk about the structure of an offshore oil rig. Study the diagram and think about the labels. Then listen and label the diagram.

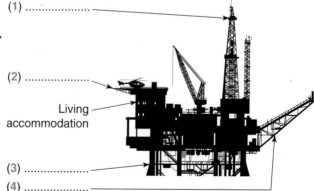

(1) ....

(2) ....

Living accommodation

(3) ....

(4) ....

Practice for the test

Section 4

 Questions 1–4

You will hear a lecture on deep sea exploration. Listen to the first part of the lecture and complete the time line using **NO MORE THAN TWO WORDS AND/OR NUMBERS.**

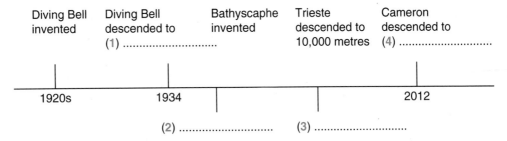

 Questions 5–8

Now you will hear the next part of the lecture. Label the diagram of the Deep Sea Challenger. Write **NO MORE THAN THREE WORDS.**

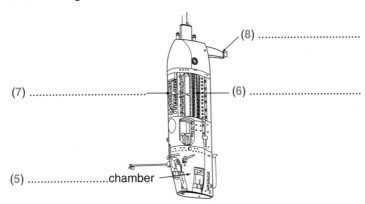

Questions 9–10

 Now listen to the final part of the lecture and complete the notes. Write **NO MORE THAN THREE WORDS OR A NUMBER.**

Justifications for deep sea research:

a Scientists understand more about the **(9)** ....
   • helps to predict earthquakes

b Increased knowledge of availability of **(10)** ....
   • commercial benefits

Describing a process for Task 1

Develop your exam skills

info For Task 1 you may have to describe a physical process. This may be illustrated in the form of a diagram showing the different steps or stages in the process. In a process description some verbs will be in the passive and some in the active.

1 **Look at the diagram. Put the sentences a–h in the correct order, 1–8.**

a The pollution is carried to the sea by rivers.

b Pollution is stored in clouds and falls as acid rain.

c Sea life and fish are killed by polluted water.

d Factories produce gas pollution and liquid pollution.

e Gas pollution rises into the air.

f Liquid pollution is also produced by factories.

g This acid rain can damage plants and animals in the countryside.

h Liquid pollution is pumped into nearby rivers.

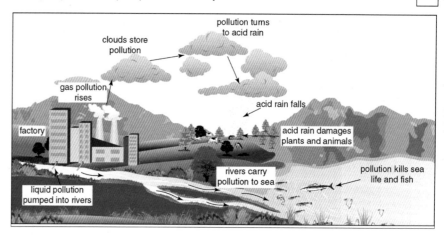

2 **Look at the labelled diagram and notes on page 61. Use the labels and the notes to write full sentences that describe the process of a volcanic eruption.**

To describe a process, you can expand the labels from a diagram into full sentences. These may be active sentences or they can be passive. Look at these examples from Exercise 1:

Label: *Rivers carry pollution to sea* **Full sentence:** *Pollution is carried to the sea by rivers.*

Label: *Clouds store pollution / pollution turns to acid rain / acid rain falls*

Full sentence: *Pollution is stored in clouds and falls as acid rain.*

Notice that the labels often do not include articles (e.g. *a, the*) or prepositions (e.g. *in, on, at*) and some labels are just nouns or verbs. You will need to use these to write full sentences – subject + verb (+ object) – and add any other words that are necessary.

1 during / eruption / magma rises / volcano's main vent

During an eruption magma rises up the volcano's main vent.

2 magma / erupt from / crater / top / volcano

3 magma / change into / lava

4 ash cloud / form / above / volcano

5 lava flows down / side / volcano

6 many trees / killed / lava

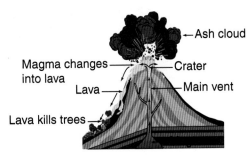

←Ash cloud

Magma changes into lava — Crater

Lava — Main vent

Lava kills trees

see **GRAMMAR** page 155 and more **PRACTICE** online

3 **Look at the diagram below. Complete the text with words that show sequence, for example, *first, first of all, secondly, next, then, (and then), when, after* and *finally*.**

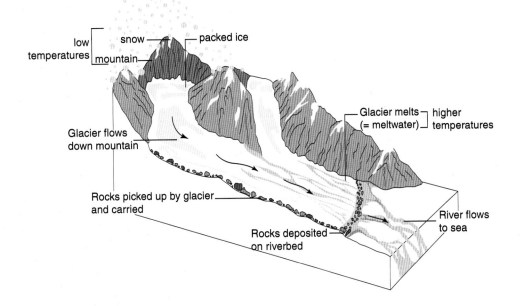

low temperatures | snow — packed ice
mountain —

Glacier melts ┐ higher
(= meltwater) ┘ temperatures

Glacier flows down mountain

Rocks picked up by glacier and carried

Rocks deposited on riverbed

River flows to sea

This diagram shows how a glacier is formed and how it moves and changes. (1) .... a large amount of snow falls on the top of a mountain. Because the temperature at the top of the mountain is very low, this snow never melts. (2) .... more snow falls on top of it, the snow turns to ice. Eventually, a lot of ice is packed together, and (3) .... it forms a glacier. The glacier becomes very heavy and it starts to move slowly down the mountain.

4 **Write more sentences to complete the description in Exercise 3. Remember to include some active and some passive verbs.**

Practice for the test

Task 1

You should spend about 20 minutes on this task.

The diagrams show the greenhouse effect on the temperature of the Earth. Describe the process.

Write at least 150 words.

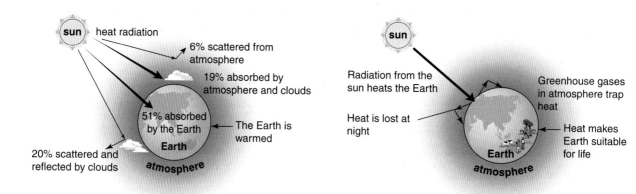

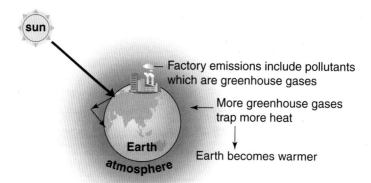

Get READY for class!

Remember to do your preparation before class.

online • workbook

see **GRAMMAR** page 155 and more **PRACTICE** online

Develop your exam skills

info

In the exam, you may be asked to read a passage and use words from it to complete labels on a diagram or picture. The answers will often come from a particular section of the passage and may not be in the same order as the questions.

1 **Look at the four questions below and think about how you will find the information in the text that follows. Then skim-read the text to find the answers to the questions as quickly as you can.**

What do jellyfish look like?

How are fossils formed?

What are barnacles?

How are seashells formed?

The beach, a natural treasure trove

When you are walking on the beach, you may be able to spot tracks. Birds and crabs leave footprints behind, especially in wet sand. On sandy beaches you will also be able to find interesting holes made by crabs that were digging for food in the mud.

You may also come across jellyfish as these are often washed up on the beach. They have no eyes, ears, heart or head and are mostly made of water. They look like a bag with arms, which are called tentacles. These contain poison that helps them catch food. Even when jellyfish are out of the water or in pieces, their tentacles may sting.

Other animals you may find are coral and barnacles. The latter are marine animals related to crabs and lobsters and live in shallow waters. They like to attach themselves to hard materials, so you are likely to find them stuck to pieces of wood.

If you are lucky, you may find a fossil. In essence, this is an animal that died and got buried in a sea bed. Fossils are likely to look like pieces of rock with an imprint of an animal skeleton. Their history is very interesting. For an animal to become fossilized, it has to be buried in mud, sand or soil; if a dead animal is not buried, it is more likely to rot away or be eaten by another animal. Over millions of years, the animal remains become buried deeper and deeper; the mud, sand or soil compresses and slowly becomes rock. The bone or shell of the animal starts to crystallize because of surrounding minerals and chemicals. Ideally, the temperature stays relatively constant throughout this process. Sometimes the fossil dissolves completely and just leaves an imprint. At other times, waves, tides and currents slowly erode the rock, which allows the animal remains to break off, ready for you to find.

What you will definitely find on a beach are shells. These were once the homes of animals such as snails or mussels, consisting of a hard layer that the animal created for protection as part of its body. After the animal has died, its soft parts have rotted or been eaten by other animals. What is left is a beautiful seashell for you to admire.

Exam tip

In the exam you may have to complete labels of pictures, diagrams, flow charts, etc. so it helps if you can think visually. If you do not have a visual imagination, start practising by trying to visually represent written information where possible.

2 **Using NO MORE THAN FOUR WORDS from the passage, complete each gap in the diagram.**

a

A dead fish is covered in (**1**) ....

b

The fish goes (**2**) .... into the soil.

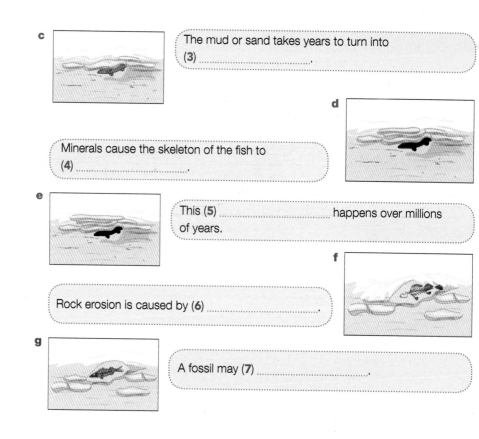

c The mud or sand takes years to turn into (**3**) ....

d Minerals cause the skeleton of the fish to (**4**) ....

e This (**5**) .... happens over millions of years.

f Rock erosion is caused by (**6**) ....

g A fossil may (**7**) ....

Practice for the test

Using **NO MORE THAN TWO WORDS** from the passage, complete each gap in the diagram.

The many uses of the Moringa tree

The Moringa tree, Saragwa, or Drumstick tree, is relatively unknown in the West despite the fact that it is incredibly useful. Miriam Tayne reports about its culinary, medicinal and other uses.

The Moringa tree is a relatively small tree that typically grows to between three and ten metres tall. Its flowers are creamy-coloured and have been compared to small orchids. The plant has long green pods that can grow up to 30 centimetres and which look a bit like drumsticks, hence the tree's common name. The pods contain round, dark brown seeds. The tree is propagated by planting the seeds or cuttings in sand or muddy soil. It does not tolerate frost but thrives in hot climates. It is very common in South and South-east Asia, Africa and America.

The leaves are reputed to have anti-inflammatory and anti-bacterial properties and so are used for eye and ear infections, fevers, etc. They are also held against the forehead to reduce headaches, or made into tea to treat stomach complaints. As they contain a lot of iron, they have been used for the treatment of anaemia, a medical condition in which there are too few red cells in the blood, causing tiredness. The plant also contains many other nutrients, such as phosphorus, calcium, potassium and vitamins A and C.

The ground-up seeds are commonly used to treat certain skin infections but can be used for much more. Ground seeds can be mixed with salt or oils and applied to the body to treat cramp, backache and forms of arthritis, a medical condition in which the joints are swollen and painful. The oil, called Ben oil because it contains behenic acid, is also used as a hair treatment or a perfume, and to deter mosquitoes and treat their bites. The by-products of the oil manufacturing process are used as a fertilizer and in water purification.

The roots work in exactly the same way as the seeds, but are much stronger, so are not used as often. They have additional uses for heart and circulation problems, whereas the gum is sometimes used to treat asthma. The bark has quite a pleasant taste and is sometimes eaten to encourage digestion.

The plant's main use, however, is as food for livestock and human beings because it contains high concentrations of fibre and protein. The drumsticks are eaten in soup or as vegetables, like green beans, and often in combination with shrimps (see picture), whereas the seeds are eaten like peas or roasted. The leaves are eaten fresh or cooked in similar ways to spinach. Chopped, they are used as a garnish on soups and salads.

They are often pickled or dried so that they are always available to use in sauces, stir-fries, soups and in sweet and sour or spicy curries.

Like every other part of the tree, the decorative flowers are also useful. They taste a bit like wild mushrooms and are considered a delicacy. They are used to make tea to treat the common cold and mixed with honey to make cough medicine.

All parts of the Moringa are used, which makes it one of the most beneficial trees in the world.

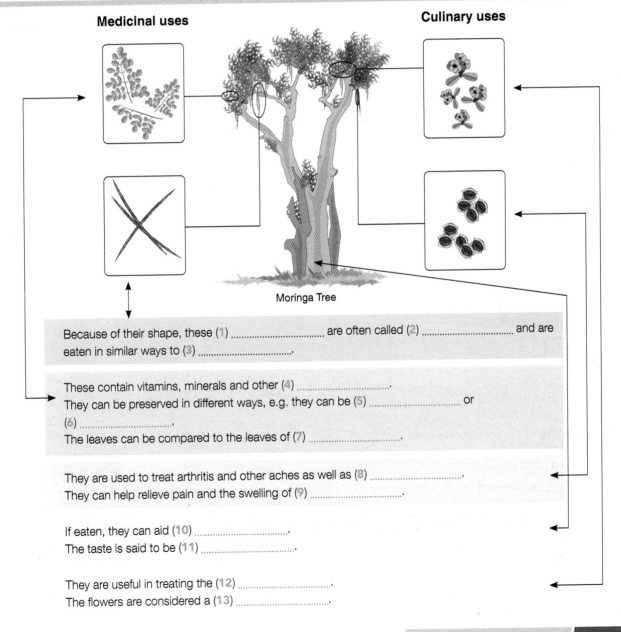

Medicinal uses

Culinary uses

Moringa Tree

Because of their shape, these (1) .... are often called (2) .... and are eaten in similar ways to (3) ....

These contain vitamins, minerals and other (4) ....
They can be preserved in different ways, e.g. they can be (5) .... or
(6) ....
The leaves can be compared to the leaves of (7) ....

They are used to treat arthritis and other aches as well as (8) ....
They can help relieve pain and the swelling of (9) ....

If eaten, they can aid (10) ....
The taste is said to be (11) ....

They are useful in treating the (12) ....
The flowers are considered a (13) ....

Unit 7

Education

Writing

Analysing and describing a bar chart for Task 1

Get READY for class!

Remember to do your preparation before class.

online • workbook

Develop your exam skills

info

For Task 1 of the Writing test you may need to describe a bar chart. Bar charts are useful for comparing the quantities of different categories (shown in the form of bars). Bar charts usually show the numbers or percentages on the left-hand vertical axis and the different categories that are being measured along the horizontal or bottom axis (plural: axes). Both axes are labelled to show what they refer to. Sometimes each category along the horizontal axis can be divided into two further sub-groups, e.g. boys / girls, so that these different sub-groups can be compared.

1 **Look at the written information about primary students and the same information in the bar chart. Answer the questions about the bar chart.**

Exam pass rates in Wales in 2003

Maths: 75,000 boys, 56,000 girls
English: 48,000 boys, 62,000 girls
Science: 59,000 boys, 46,000 girls

History: 35,000 boys, 44,000 girls
Geography: 28,000 boys, 46,000 girls
Art: 41,000 boys, 55,000 girls

Exam pass rates in Wales, 2003

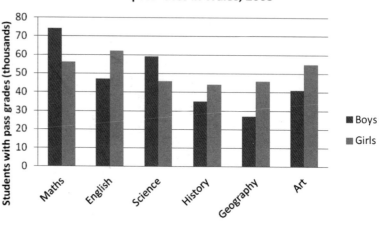

1 What do the numbers on the vertical axis measure?

2 How is the information grouped on the horizontal axis?

3 What do the different shades of the bars show?

4 When was the data collected?

2 **Look at the bar chart in Exercise 1 again. Read the introduction to a text about the bar chart. Complete the paragraph about the girls using the phrases below.**

> ~~60 thousand~~   more   40 thousand   English
>
> Geography   20 thousand   History   Art

This bar chart shows the numbers (in thousands) of students with pass grades in different subject exams in Wales in 2003. The chart groups the students according to subject and divides these subject groups into boys and girls. There are clear differences between the boys and the girls.

Similar numbers of girls achieved pass grades in all the subjects. The number of girls with pass grades ranged from the highest number of just over (1) *60 thousand* to the lowest number of just over (2) .... , a difference of around (3) .... Girls did best in Art, Maths and (4) .... , while their lowest pass rate was in (5) .... Girls achieved (6) .... passes than boys in four subjects: English, (7) .... , History and (8) ....

Practice for the test

Task 1

You should spend about 20 minutes on this task.

The bar chart below shows the number of students who chose certain university subjects in 2005. Summarize the information by selecting and reporting the main features, and make comparisons where relevant.

Write at least 100 words.

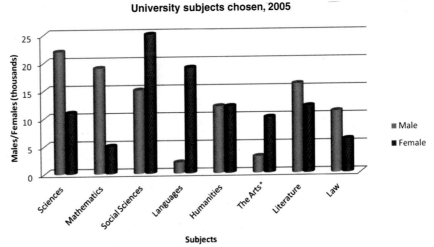

University subjects chosen, 2005

'The Arts' = subjects like Art, Music, Drama

Speaking

Using a range of vocabulary to express clear opinions in Parts 2 and 3

Get READY for class!

Remember to do your preparation before class.

online • workbook

Develop your exam skills

info

In Part 2, you talk for one to two minutes about the task card. Then the examiner asks you one or two questions related to your answer, and this completes Part 2. These questions test your ability to give a relevant answer with a range of vocabulary.

🎧 48 1 Imagine you have completed your two-minute talk on the Part 2 task card below. The examiner will ask you one more question. Listen to an example answer. Which question, 1 or 2, does it answer?

> **Talk about a subject you are studying.**
>
> You should say:
>
> what subject you are studying
> what the subject is about
> how you feel about it
>
> and explain why you are interested in it.

1 Would you like a job connected to the subject you are studying?

2 Are your friends or family interested in the subject too?

see GRAMMAR page 142 and more PRACTICE online

🎧 48 2 Read and listen to the example answer again. Write T (true) or F (false) for sentences 1–3 below.

> Yes, yes they are. My father and my brother studied law at university, and they think it is a very nice subject. My mother thinks it is nice and always asks me questions about law. I have lots of friends on the course, and we want to get a nice job when we graduate.

1 The answer is relevant to the topic. ....

2 The answer includes all parts of the question. ....

3 The speaker repeats some words. ....

Exam tip

Use a range of appropriate adjectives in the exam. Try not to repeat words even when you want to say something similar, for example, *good*, *great*, *wonderful*. However, remember that words rarely mean exactly the same thing, for example, *great* and *wonderful* are a bit stronger than *good*.

3 Look at the example answer in Exercise 2 again. Underline the three adjectives and replace each adjective with one of the adjectives below.

> good   important   interesting

🎧 49 4 Listen and check. Assess the answer again using sentences 1–3 in Exercise 2. Which answer has changed?

info

Part 3 tests your ability to express your opinion in a clear way and to use relevant language and a range of vocabulary.

see GRAMMAR
page 145 and more
PRACTICE online

5 **Record your answers to the questions in Exercise 1. Use the questions below to check your answer. Use the questions to check your partner's answer.**

- Are your answers relevant to the topic?
- Do you answer all parts of the question?
- Do you repeat any words?
- How many different adjectives do you use?

 6 **You will hear three people answering the three questions below. Read the questions and match each one to a speaker 1–3.**

a Is it a good idea to live with your family when you are studying? ....

b Compare your experience of education to your parents' generation. ....

c Do you think your country has a good education system? ....

7 **Record your answers to the questions in Exercise 6. Read the sentences below and write T (true) or F (false) to assess your answers. Then check your partner's answer.**

1 The answer is four or more sentences long. ....

2 The answer is relevant to the topic. ....

3 The answer includes a range of adjectives and adverbs. ....

Practice for the test

Part 1

 1 **Listen to five Part 1 questions. Record your answer to each question.**

Part 2

2 **Read the Part 2 task card.
Plan your answer. You have
one minute for this in the exam.
Then record your answer.
You have one to two minutes
for this in the exam.**

> **Talk about a subject you are studying.**
>
> You should say:
>
> which subject you are studying
> what the subject is about
> how you feel about it
>
> and explain why you are interested in it.

Exam tip

Remember to
include other relevant
grammar, like the
past simple and the
present simple.

3 **Answer the question below to
complete Part 2. Record your
answer.**

Would you like a job related to this subject?

Part 3

4 **Listen to five Part 3 questions. Answer two of the questions and record
your answer.**

Get READY for class!

Remember to do your preparation before class.

online • workbook

Develop your exam skills

info

In the exam, you may be given a table or a flow chart (a series of steps linked by arrows) with gaps in it. You will need to read a passage to find the missing information. The answers may be in one particular section of the text, but are unlikely to be in the same order as the gaps. You will be told how many words from the text you should use, e.g. *no more than two words and/or a number, one word only*.

Exam tip

Remember that scanning the text (moving your eyes down it quickly to find specific information) saves time when you read. The following four exercises help you practise scanning. They all refer to the text on page 71.

1 Look at the text *Is it better to go abroad to study*? Read the headings to understand the organization of the text. Decide which paragraph(s) you would need to read properly if you only wanted to find out about the reasons why people choose to study abroad.

Paragraph number(s): ....

2 Scan the text again to find names of countries, people and organizations. Complete the table.

Countries	People	Organizations or institutions

Exam tip

Use the text style or formatting to help you find the information in the text that you are looking for, e.g. uppercase letters, numbers, italics, bold print, quotation marks and other visual information.

3 For this exercise, scan the text again in one minute if you can. Scan the text for the different items in the table. Feed back as a class. See how long it takes to find any information you missed.

Numbers	
Words in italics	
Words in bold print	
Abbreviations	

see **GRAMMAR** page 153 and more **PRACTICE** online

4 **Scan the text quickly again to answer the following questions.**

1 Which paragraph(s) give(s) somebody's opinion?

2 What does somebody really want people to understand?

3 Which two paragraphs talk about the country that is the most welcoming to overseas students?

4 Which paragraph gives examples to explain what an internationalization approach is?

5 **Think about what you did in Exercises 1 to 4. How did you find the answers without reading the text in detail? How can this help you in the exam?**

Is it better to go abroad to study?

Student-friendly places

The British Council has named the universities that are most welcoming to overseas students. As you would expect, English-speaking countries such as Australia, the UK and the US have made the top 10, but the number one may be a surprise: Germany. Two Far Eastern countries, i.e. China and Malaysia, made it to the top 5, ranking higher than the US, Japan, Russia, Nigeria and Brazil.

The benefits of studying abroad

Russell Howe, a Scot who is currently studying for a Business degree at Stellinga International College in the Netherlands, previously also studied in India (which came 11th on the list). 'People often ask me why I needed to travel, because British universities have a good reputation elsewhere in the world. But this is not something I *needed* to do, but something I really *wanted* to do. I have learnt different ways of looking at things, but I also found out how much we all have in common, wherever we are from. All of this will be useful in my future career.'

Russell is not the only international student in his department. Business and administrative courses are the most popular with international students, followed by engineering and technology, social studies, creative arts and design, medicine-related topics and law. Manal, a student at the Faculty of Art and Design at Stellinga, says she has similar reasons to Russell, but there is more: 'I wanted to broaden my understanding of the world. I have enhanced my language skills: I am more fluent in English and have also taken a level 1 Dutch evening class. One of my modules is about European art, and I believe that I am benefiting more from studying this in Europe than anywhere else. I have managed to visit other countries in my holidays, and really feel that this whole experience is developing my global perspective. I also hope that I have made lasting friendships and contacts.'

Enabling student access

What is it that makes these countries student-friendly? Well, all of them make it easy for international students to apply and provide ongoing support once they are there. They also offer good quality degrees, which are valued highly in other countries too. The fact that Germany came out as winner is probably due to the country's efforts towards *internationalization*. One aspect of this is that the country welcomes foreign students by charging them the same fees as home students, meaning that in some universities overseas students study for free. Many classes are conducted in English, and most leaflets are in English too, making it easier for international students to keep informed and take part in student life.

Apart from the financial reasons already mentioned, this type of educational internationalization can help with the quality of research in these universities, e.g. through networking, team work and the sharing of skills. For students, it is a valuable addition to their skills and experience at a time when jobs are not easy to find.

Glossary

British Council: an organization that connects people worldwide with learning opportunities and creative ideas from the UK

Practice for the test

Questions 1–11

Using **NO MORE THAN TWO WORDS** from the passage for each answer, complete the table and the flow chart below.

The required documents:

Evidence of language ability	IELTS 6.5 or (1) ....
Evidence of studies	(2) .... , Dutch VWO diploma, or other secondary school diploma
Information about motivation	(3) .... with a maximum length of (4) ....
Proof of identity	(5) .... and passport photo
Other	(6) .... if originals are in a foreign language

The online application process for people outside the EU:

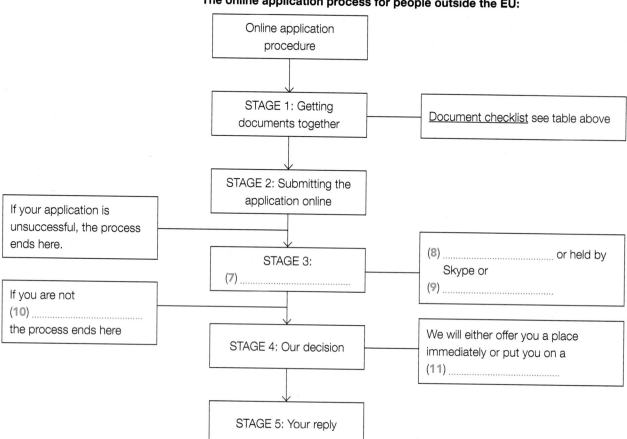

```
┌─────────────────────────┐
│   Online application    │
│       procedure         │
└───────────┬─────────────┘
            ↓
┌─────────────────────────┐        ┌──────────────────────────────────┐
│   STAGE 1: Getting      │────────│ Document checklist see table above │
│   documents together    │        └──────────────────────────────────┘
└───────────┬─────────────┘
            ↓
┌─────────────────────────┐
│  STAGE 2: Submitting the│
│   application online    │
└───────────┬─────────────┘
            ↓
┌──────────────────────┐   ┌───────────────┐   ┌──────────────────────────────┐
│ If your application is│───│   STAGE 3:    │───│ (8) .................. or held by │
│ unsuccessful, the     │   │ (7) .......... │   │    Skype or                  │
│ process ends here.    │   └───────┬───────┘   │ (9) .......................... │
└──────────────────────┘           │           └──────────────────────────────┘
┌──────────────────────┐           │
│ If you are not        │──────────┤
│ (10) ................. │          │
│ the process ends here │          ↓
└──────────────────────┘   ┌───────────────┐   ┌──────────────────────────────┐
                           │ STAGE 4: Our  │───│ We will either offer you a place │
                           │   decision    │   │ immediately or put you on a  │
                           └───────┬───────┘   │ (11) .......................... │
                                   │           └──────────────────────────────┘
                                   ↓
                           ┌───────────────┐
                           │ STAGE 5: Your │
                           │    reply      │
                           └───────────────┘
```

Get READY for class!
Remember to do your preparation before class.
online • workbook

Develop your exam skills

In Section 3 of the Listening test you will hear a group of people talking about a topic related to education or training. You will be asked to do different tasks in this section, and some of these will require you to identify the ideas and opinions of the individual speakers.

1 Look at the following sentence beginnings and sentence endings. Discuss the options. For each question more than one answer is possible. Choose the endings that are grammatically correct.

1 *Your exam revision will be more organized at the end of the year if*
  a you are planning a revision timetable.
  b you plan when to study each subject.
  c your revision is planning.
  d you have planned a revision timetable.

2 *Some subjects are easier to remember because*
  a they interesting.
  b they are interested.
  c they are interesting.
  d you are interested in them.

3 *If you study all night because it is quieter,*
  a you will be tired in the morning.
  b you are sleeping in your classes.
  c you might fall asleep in your lectures.
  d you will be able to concentrate more.

Exam tip

When you are listening to a recording of several people talking, try to make a note of the names of the speakers when you hear them for the first time. It might help you to write just their initials and whether they are male or female. For example: *A / f* (Amira – female) or *D / m* (Dave – male).

 2 You will hear a conversation about studying. Listen and identify the gender of each student. Listen again and match the name of each person to the study technique they prefer.

1 Martha .... 2 Carl .... 3 Enrique .... 4 Jenny ....

A highlighting important details in photocopies of articles and text books
B writing notes in an exercise book
C making notes in files on their PC
D using free software to make notes on articles and electronic books

 3 You will hear a group of students talking about their revision techniques. First predict possible endings to each sentence. Then listen to the recording and write the correct endings for the sentences. Write **NO MORE THAN THREE WORDS**.

1 Lesley prepares for her end-of-year exams by making a

....

2 Chen says that he can remember facts more easily if he creates pictures

....

3 Indira prefers to study late at night because it is ....

4 Mark likes to get up very early on the day of an exam to do some

....

 4 You will hear a student talking to a receptionist about what do when going for an exam. First look at the pictures and predict what the instructions will be. Then listen to the recording and complete the instructions. Write **NO MORE THAN THREE WORDS** for each answer. Check that your answers are grammatically correct.

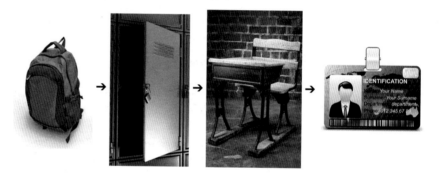

1 Leave your .... your bag.

2 The keys for the lockers are ....

3 Show your identity card ....

4 Look for your .... on a desk in the hall.

5 The following steps about preparing for an exam are in the wrong order. Put the steps in the order you would do them. There are several possible answers, but some are more practical than others. Don't check your answers yet.

A look at past exam papers

B read all the books on the subject

C write practice exam questions

D remember key facts and arguments

E discuss possible exam topics with tutors

F look at all your lecture notes for the course

 6 You will hear three students talking about how they prepare for an exam. Complete the flow chart with the missing letters from Exercise 5.

(1) .... → (2) .... → **D** → (3) .... → (4) ....

If you don't hear the
answer to a question
and you are unable
to answer it, don't
waste time worrying
about it. Go on and
listen for the answer
to the next question.
At the end, go back
and try to guess the
answers that you
missed. You might be
able to get an extra
mark or two. If you
leave them blank, you
definitely won't get a
mark!

Practice for the test

Section 3

 Questions 1–4

You will hear three students discussing exam techniques with their tutor.
Complete the flow chart. Write **NO MORE THAN THREE WORDS**.

> Make sure you have the (**1**) ....

> Write (**2**) ....

> Read (**3**) ....

> Check that you know (**4**) .... the exam is.

Questions 5–8

Now you will hear the next part of the recording. Complete the sentences.
Write **NO MORE THAN THREE WORDS** for each answer.

5 You should read the questions .... to find out what
the topic is.

6 Sometimes a question is .... than it looks.

7 It is a good idea to start by answering the questions you
....

8 When all the questions are worth the same .... ,
you should check that you spend the right amount of time on them.

Questions 9–10

Listen to the last part of the recording and answer the questions. Write **NO
MORE THAN THREE WORDS OR A NUMBER**.

9 What should you write if you do not have time to give a complete answer to
a question? ....

10 What did Barbara get in her last exam?
....

Unit 8

Work

Get READY for class!

Remember to do your preparation before class.

online • workbook

Develop your exam skills

info In Section 4 of the Listening test you will hear one person talking about an academic topic of general interest. You may have to complete a summary or notes, or give short answers to questions.

1 Speakers often introduce the topic of a lecture with one of the phrases below. Think about which two you would be most likely to use yourself and why.

> Today I'm going to talk about …

> My lecture this evening will be about …

> My topic today is …

> In today's lecture I'll be talking about …

🎧60 **2** You will hear four introductions to different talks. Think about how to complete the topics of the talks below. Then listen and write / complete the topic of each talk.

1 .... you can join at university

2 working in ....

3 jobs that involve spending a lot of time ....

4 employment opportunities in ....

3 Some of the words below have similar meanings to the lecture topics in Exercise 2. Find two words or phrases with similar meanings to each topic.

> in the open air   enjoyment   employment   associations   business   outside
> colleges   fulfilment   universities   company   occupation   clubs   work

1 ....   3 ....   5 ....

2 ....   4 ....   6 ....

🎧61 **4** You will hear six very similar introductions. Listen to how they are different. Listen again and complete the sentences with ONE word only.

1 .... you can join at university

2 working in a small ....

3 jobs that involve spending a lot of time ....

4 employment in ....

Exam tip

Before you listen to each part of the lecture in Section 4, read the questions carefully and underline the key words. This will give you some information about the topic in advance and help you focus on the main ideas while you are listening.

see **GRAMMAR** page 146 and get more **PRACTICE** online

5 You will hear two interviews with people about work. Listen and complete the notes. Write **NO MORE THAN TWO WORDS** for each answer.

Alice works on (**1**) ....
– grows (**2**) ....
– keeps (**3**) ...., ducks and cows
– worst part of job – going out in winter to feed (**4**) ....
– likes working outdoors in the (**5**) ....
– trucks deliver to (**6**) ....
– supplies (**7**) ....with milk

Wei Long works as a (**8**) ....
– graduated in (**9**) ....
– ambition: earn living through (**10**) ....
– has own (**11**) ....
– sells (**12**) ....
– (**13**) ....looks after the office
– likes making own (**14**) ....
– wouldn't like to work in a (**15**) ....

Practice for the test

Section 4

Questions 1–4

You will hear a woman talking about her job. Complete the notes with words from the recording. Write **NO MORE THAN TWO WORDS** for each answer.

Job: (**1**) .... for five years

Studied: (**2**) .... at university

Interested in (**3**) .... side, not theory

Accepted for (**4**) .... after graduating

Questions 5–7

Now you will hear the next part of the recording. Answer the question. Choose **THREE** answers from a–f.

What does the speaker think are the disadvantages of police work?

a danger of being attacked

b protecting the public

c not being available for family celebrations

d special training in avoiding trouble

e working difficult hours

f working with the public

5 ....   6 ....   7 ....

Questions 8–10

Listen to the last part of the recording and answer the questions. Write **NO MORE THAN TWO WORDS**.

8 What does the speaker think about the financial rewards of police work?

....

9 What kind of people do the police sometimes have to protect? ....

10 What does the speaker want to be in the future? ....

have to • using phrases to give you time to think

Develop your exam skills

info The Speaking test assesses your ability to speak coherently (to give answers that are easy to follow and understand) and fluently (to keep talking without repeating words and without pauses).

1 **Read the Part 3 questions below. Underline the key words. How do they help you understand the question?**

1 Compare your experience of finding a job to your parents' generation.

2 Many people think that work experience is the best way to learn about a job. What is your point of view?

3 In your opinion, do people work more now than in the past?

4 Do you think companies need people to travel to an office and work there, or can people work from home?

2 **Read the Part 3 questions again. Which questions ask you to …**

a give your opinion on an issue?

b compare the past to the present?

3 **Read the example answer below (ignoring the gaps). Which question from Exercise 1 is it answering? How do you know?**

That's an (1) .... **question. Let me (2)** .... I definitely think that work experience is an important way to learn about a job. I studied business for three years and I graduated with honours. Then I got a good job, but it was really hard work and tiring. **I (3)** .... **that** your first job is always difficult. I learnt lots in my first year there. But my course did help me. For example, I understood lots of basic points about business and finance. **There are pros and (4)** .... Work experience is an excellent way to learn about a job in real life, but education or training gives you time to learn the theories.

Exam tip

Including useful phrases in your answers gives you time to think and relax in the test. It also shows the examiner you are speaking at a natural pace and without pauses.

 4 **You will hear a student giving the answer in Exercise 3. Look at the bold phrases in Exercise 3 and think about how to complete the gaps. Then listen and complete the gaps in the phrases. How do the useful phrases help the speaker and improve the answer?**

 5 **You will hear another example answer. Listen and tick the question it answers from Exercise 1. Then listen again and complete the useful phrases below.**

1 That's ....

2 Let me ....

3 I .... that .... …

4 I'm not ....

5 There are advantages and

....

see **GRAMMAR** page 159 and more **PRACTICE** online

6 **Look back at question 2 in Exercise 1. Think about your answer and which relevant useful phrases you can include. Record your answer.**

7 Listen to your answer. Does it sound natural? How could you improve it? Record your answer again.

 8 You will hear two Part 3 questions. Listen and answer the questions below.

a Do you have to give your opinion on an issue, or compare past and present?

b Which useful phrases can you include?

 9 Close your book and listen to the two Part 3 questions again. Record your answer after each one.

10 Listen and assess your answers using the questions below. Then practise giving your answers again.

1 Do the answers sound natural?

2 How many pauses are there?

3 How many useful phrases are there?

Exam tip

In Part 3, you can ask the examiner to repeat the question if you don't understand or if you don't hear. Say: *Can you repeat the question, please?*

see **GRAMMAR** page 146 and more **PRACTICE** online

Practice for the test

Part 1

1 Read the Part 1 questions. Record your answer to each question.

1 What do you do?

2 Do you enjoy your work? Why / Why not?

3 Is there another type of work you would like to do?

4 Describe the company or organization you work for.

5 Describe a typical day in your job.

Part 2

2 Read the Part 2 task card. Plan your answer. You have one minute for this in the exam. Then record your answer. You have one to two minutes for this in the exam.

> **Describe a job you have now or had in the past.**
>
> You should say:
>
> how you got the job
> what the job involves
> why you wanted the job
>
> and describe how well you do or did the job.

3 Answer the question below to complete Part 2. Record your answer.

What are / were your colleagues like?

Part 3

4 Read the Part 3 questions. Answer two of the questions and record your answer.

1 In your opinion, is it a good idea for families to work together?

2 Many people think that work experience is the best way to learn about a job. What is your point of view?

3 In your opinion, do people work more now than in the past?

4 Do you think working from home is a good idea?

Completing notes and summaries

Develop your exam skills

info

In the IELTS exam, you may be given a summary of, or notes about, a text, but there will be information missing which you will have to look for. You will usually find the information in a particular part of the text, but not in the same order. You will either have to choose words from the text or choose the correct option from those given.

Exam tip

It is often easier to choose the correct answer if you can predict the type of word you need by using your knowledge of grammar.

1 Copy and complete the table. Write the words below under the correct part of speech.

> satellite   mobile   newspaper   transfer   broadband   fast   consumer   access
> free   speedy   handy   keyboard   signal   commercial

Adjectives	Nouns	Verbs	Adverbs

2 Read the example explanation of how to predict possible answers. Complete the five remaining sentences using a process similar to the example.

1 Websites allow us to .... a library's catalogue of books and periodicals. *The structure is allow somebody to do (verb) something.* There are a number of possibilities, e.g. *access, consult, preview, see.*

2 Public libraries are changing. You can still borrow and .... books, magazines, DVDs, CDs and other media.

3 *Communication* refers to both the act of .... , in other words the exchange of information, ideas or feelings, and something that is ....' for example a letter or telephone call.

4 DVDs aren't just for films anymore. New DVDs (digital video discs) provide even .... sound quality than audio CDs (compact discs).

5 Both CDs and DVDs sample the music, but DVDs are able to .... more information and they have more samples per second. The information is also more ....

6 After 1066, many French and Latin words came .... the English language.

3 Scan the first two paragraphs of the text on page 81 and find the missing words to complete the notes. Do the notes contain the key information from the two paragraphs?

> • _____ *types of communication:*
> • _____ **(1)** ....   ⎫
> • _____ **(2)** ... *written* ......   ⎬ *verbal*
> • _____ **(3)** ....   ⎭

In all communication, whether this is verbal or non-verbal, a sender transfers a message to a receiver, choosing a certain medium. The receiver uses the message clues and the context, and decodes it to understand it. This is often followed by a new message in return, and so the communication process continues.

Although this procedure is always the same, it can take many different forms depending on the type of communication. For example, in non-verbal communication (as opposed to written and spoken communication, which are both verbal), the code used could be gestures, body language, eye contact and facial expressions, such as a smile.

Communication is extremely important in the business world and in this context both informal and formal styles will be used. However, there are still clear rules that should be followed. If we take the example of meetings, they are often conducted in quite a relaxed way, with participants using first names and informal language. However, as soon as the meeting is official, careful written records will be kept, called minutes. Like reports, these will follow a format that is standard across many business situations. One important aspect is layout. Another aspect is content, and this will depend to some extent on the level of formality. Annual business reports must include certain types of information to be legal, e.g. financial information, but even a simple letter would not function as it should without the use of somebody's title (e.g. *Mr or Ms*). Language is another aspect which needs to be taken into account. Business communication, when written, needs to be clear and to the point, without spelling or grammar mistakes. Not following these important rules would have a negative effect in any business context.

4 Look at the summary of the text in Exercise 3. Think about the grammatical category for each of the missing words. Re-read the text and look for suitable words to complete the summary.

It is important to follow the rules when communicating in writing, especially if you are in the world of (**1**) .... There are three areas which are important: (**2**) ...., content and language. The language can be formal or (**3**) .... but there should be no mistakes. You cannot just choose to include what you like, for example (**4**) .... information must be included in annual business (**5**) .... Business writing also needs to look good on the page, with everything written in a (**6**) .... format.

Practice for the test

1 Answer the following questions about the passage below within two minutes. Use words from the passage for your answers. Note that these questions follow the order of the information in the text and have no word limit (just for this exercise).

1 Name a complaint that is often made about managers in the United Kingdom.

2 What is the cause of the loss of international business?

3 What is a requirement for managers to do a good job?

4 Which groups of people outside their company do managers have to communicate with?

One criticism of UK managers is that relatively few speak a second language fluently. This can cause obvious problems for businesses that trade in a global market. Research suggests that UK companies lose around 13 per cent of the international deals they try to complete due to 'communication problems'. Managers also need effective written skills if they are to carry out their jobs effectively. The ability to quickly summarize key points in the form of a report for others in the business is of real value. So is the skill of reading a report written by someone else and being able to draw out the important elements.

As well as their own staff, managers have to work with other people too. They interact with customers, more senior managers, suppliers, trade union officials, government officials and the local community. Managers need to be comfortable in the company of diverse groups, and they need to be able to communicate formally when required and to engage in informal small talk.

2 Complete summaries A and B with words from the corresponding passages below. Write **NO MORE THAN ONE WORD** for each answer.

Summary A

There should be a small number of (**1**) .... management and clarity about what the meeting at meetings and there needs to be a (**2**) .... should hopefully (**4**) .... At the end, for any meeting, which will include a clear agenda. During there should be a summary and agreement about the meeting there needs to be good (**3**) .... (**5**) .... action.

Passage A

Managers need a range of communication skills to carry out their jobs effectively. They need to be able to articulate their ideas and vision and to convey enthusiasm. Good managers may, at times, need to be able to argue points cogently and to persuade people to their point of view. However, good managers appreciate that communication is a two-way process, and that listening is an important element of communication. Listening to the views of others can help to test ideas as well as to develop new products and methods of production.

The most common forum in which managers are required to communicate are meetings. It is important for managers to plan for meetings, whether with a single person or with a group. Managers should not invite too many participants to keep numbers to a minimum. They should have a clear agenda for discussion and should exercise tight time controls to prevent meetings dragging on. Managers should enter each meeting with a clear idea of what they want it to achieve. At the end of a meeting it is good practice to summarize what has been agreed and what needs to happen in the future.

Summary B

Working with other people is not always easy, but it is (**6**) .... for the role of managers that they have interpersonal skills that are (**7**) ....

Their (**8**) .... may need encouragement and help with (**9**) .... and solving problems between colleagues.

Passage B

Communication skills should not be taken for granted. Many managers require training in written and oral communication skills and many businesses would benefit from employing managers who speak at least one other language.

Interpersonal skills are also necessary if a manager is to work successfully with other people. If managers lack interpersonal skills, then they are likely to be of limited effectiveness in their role. Managers with effective interpersonal skills can motivate others and can co-ordinate the work of their employees. To do this, managers may need to coach and encourage employees as well as solving disputes and, perhaps more importantly, preventing conflict.

Develop your exam skills

> **info**
>
> For a Task 2 essay, you may have to evaluate questions or arguments. To do this, you will need to consider advantages and disadvantages in a balanced way to show that you understand both sides.

1 **Read the list of ideas for the essay question below. Decide if the ideas are advantages or disadvantages. Write A (advantage) or D (disadvantage) next to each idea.**

What are the advantages and disadvantages of using mobile phones at work?

1 Colleagues can easily contact each other. ....

2 The charges for talking on mobile phones are very expensive. ....

3 Employees spend too much time talking to their friends on mobile phones.

4 Mobile phones are often lost or stolen. ....

5 Some employees work better if they can listen to music while they work. ....

6 Mobile phones distract employees from their work. ....

7 Employees always have a way of contacting their office when they are away.

....

8 There are many apps for mobile phones that can help employees with their work.

....

2 **Match the supporting information on the right to the ideas from Exercise 1 on the left.**

Ideas	Supporting information
1 Colleagues can easily contact each other.	a Some businesses cannot afford to pay expensive mobile phone charges.
2 The charges for talking on mobile phones are very expensive.	b It is expensive to replace them.
3 Employees spend too much time talking to their friends on mobile phones.	c They do not need to buy other types of technology
4 Mobile phones are often lost or stolen.	d They should focus on working while in the office.
5 Mobile phones distract employees from their work.	e This can help avoid problems when employees are away.
6 Children can use mobile phone technology for copying documents.	f They should spend less time chatting and more time working.

3 Match ideas a–f to paragraph functions 1–6. Then decide the best order for sentences a–f in a paragraph and write it below.

1 Main idea $\boxed{e}$ a Today, these phones are used by most people to keep in touch with friends and work.

2 Example $\boxed{}$ b Mobile phones can help managers find out where their employees are.

3 Reason $\boxed{}$ c For example, if an employee is late returning to the office, their colleagues can find out where they are.

4 Expansion $\boxed{}$ d In addition, mobile phones make arrangements easier.

5 Supporting idea 1 $\boxed{}$ e Mobile phones are an excellent tool for communication.

6 Supporting idea 2 $\boxed{}$ f This is because people can use their mobile phones to change plans or call people if they are delayed.

Paragraph order:

e ....

4 Read the essay question and the ideas below. Then put the ideas into two groups: advantages and disadvantages.

What are the advantages and disadvantages of social networking at work?

1 There is a lot of fraud online and you cannot trust your online contacts.

2 Social networking means we can keep in touch with colleagues and clients easily.

3 It is a useful way of recruiting employees without spending much money.

4 Social networking can be addictive, especially in younger employees.

5 Social networking can help businesses find out about the latest trends.

6 Employees waste time rather than working.

7 Often when a financial story breaks, social networking sites help us hear the opinions of a wide range of experts.

8 It allows employees to discuss ideas, post news and share links.

5 Use the ideas from Exercise 4 to write two paragraphs, one paragraph about advantages and one about disadvantages. Begin your two paragraphs like this:

There are many advantages of social networking. Firstly, ...

However, social networking also has some disadvantages. ...

6 Read the three essay titles below. Then write short notes listing advantages and disadvantages for each one.

1 What are the advantages and disadvantages of using data projectors at work?

2 There are more advantages than disadvantages of modern technology. How far do you agree with this statement?

3 The Internet has more advantages for young people than old people. Do you agree?

When you have described the advantages and disadvantages of a situation / argument, you can say which side has the strongest case in your opinion.

7 **Read the essay title and the first two paragraphs of the essay below. Write notes for paragraph 3 using your own ideas. Then write the paragraph including reasons and examples.**

What are the advantages and disadvantages of social networking in the workplace?

Social networking is common nowadays. There are few people who don't have an account on sites like BeBo or Facebook. However, whether people should use these sites at work is debatable. Some people say that these sites should be banned at work, while others say that they can be an advantage. I believe these sites should be used in the workplace.

Firstly, many people say social networking sites should be banned in a work environment because staff spend too much time using them when they should be working and this can have a negative effect on a company's productivity. People use these sites at work in order to keep up-to-date with news and gossip. However, many people have lost their jobs because they have used these websites too frequently or because they have said something negative about their company or their bosses on such sites.

On the other hand, these sites can also have positive aspects in the workplace. …

....

....

....

....

....

....

....

In conclusion, I believe that although there are disadvantages to using social networking in the workplace, people should be able to do it.

Practice for the test

Task 2

You should spend about 40 minutes on this task.
Write about the following topic:

The Internet has as many disadvantages as it does advantages.

To what extent do you agree with this statement?

Give reasons for your answer and include any relevant examples from your own knowledge or experience.

Write at least 250 words.

Unit 9

Holidays and travel

opposite adjectives • *be going to* • pronunciation: /ə/ and sentence stress • taking notes and preparing answers

Develop your exam skills

Get READY for class!
Remember to do your preparation before class.
online • workbook

Exam tip

Revise your vocabulary regularly and practise using it. This helps you to remember your vocabulary in the test and to use your vocabulary with the correct topics.

info The Speaking test assesses your ability to use a range of relevant vocabulary to talk about the different IELTS topics.

1 **Match the topics 1–8 to the groups of words a–h. Choose three topics and practise saying the words. Then put each word in a sentence relating to holidays.**

1 Family
2 Free time activities
3 Special occasions
4 Cities
5 TV and radio programmes
6 The weather
7 Studying
8 Work

a characters, dramatic, plots, series, soap operas
b accommodation, busy, gallery, skyscraper, traditional food
c colleague, office, part-time, salary, volunteer
d business studies, grades, literature, medicine, university
e boring, chatting online, doing nothing, meeting friends, prefer
f costume, dance, make, parade, presents
g bossy, funny, husband, look like, parents
h autumn, monsoon, November, season, snowy

2 **Use the topics in Exercise 1 to ask and answer the Part 1 questions below with your partner. Then record your answers.**

1 Do you have a large family?
2 How often do you read newspapers?
3 Do you enjoy going to special occasions?
4 Where is your hometown located?
5 What do you usually watch on television?
6 What's the weather like in your country?
7 What are you studying now?
8 What do you do?

3 **Listen to your answers and note down the vocabulary you used. Could you use more words? Answer the questions again and try to use more words.**

see **GRAMMAR** page 155 and more **PRACTICE** online

see **GRAMMAR** page 148 and more **PRACTICE** online

4 Read the Part 2 task card and plan your answer. Which words and phrases can you include to show your range of vocabulary? Which useful phrases can you include to organize your answer?

5 Record your answer in Exercise 4. Work with a partner and listen to each other's answers. Could you include more vocabulary and more useful phrases? Record your answer again and try to improve it.

> **Describe a friend that you like spending time with.**
>
> You should say:
>
> when and how you met
> how often you see this friend
> what kind of personality your friend has
>
> and say why you like spending time with this friend.

 6 You will hear a question related to the task card in Exercise 4. Listen and record your answer.

 7 You will hear four Part 3 questions. What is each question asking you to do? Write O (give your opinion) or C (compare the past to the present).

1 .... 2 .... 3 .... 4 ....

8 Look at the useful phrases below. Which ones could you include in your answers? Can you think of other useful phrases?

> I'm not sure.   Let me see.   That's interesting.   There are pros and cons.

 9 You will hear the questions in Exercise 7 again. Listen and record your answers. Then work with a partner: think about how to include more vocabulary and more useful phrases. Record your answer again and try to improve it.

Practice for the test

Part 1

 1 Listen to five Part 1 questions. Record your answer to each question.

Part 2

2 Listen to and read the Part 2 task card. Plan your answer. You have one minute for this in the exam. Then record your answer. You have one to two minutes for this in the exam.

> **Talk about a special holiday or trip.**
>
> You should say:
>
> what it was
> when and where you went
> what you did
>
> and explain why it is special to you.

3 Answer the question below to complete Part 2. Record your answer.

Are you going to go on a similar trip in the future?

Part 3

 4 Listen to four Part 3 questions. Answer the questions and record your answer.

Develop your exam skills

> **info**
>
> A line graph shows how the value of something changes over time. The vertical axis shows quantities, e.g. numbers, percentages or money. The horizontal axis shows different points in time, usually months or years. Different quantities measured at different points in time can be joined using a continuous line to show a trend or how these quantities change, e.g. increase, decrease or stay the same. More lines (different colours or styles) can be used for different categories. The key explains which categories are being measured.

Exam tip

Check the horizontal axis to find the periods of time the graph refers to: past, present, future or all three.

Use the present simple to describe the graph: *The graph shows ... , We can see ...*

If the graph refers to past periods of time, use the past simple to describe these.

If the graph refers to something that began in the past but is still happening now, use the present perfect.

If the graph includes future times, use *It is predicted that ... , ... will ...*

1 Look at the line graph. Write **T** (true) or **F** (false) next to the sentences below.

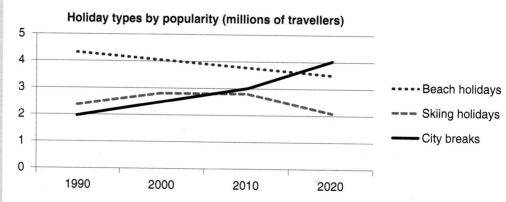

Holiday types by popularity (millions of travellers)

..... Beach holidays
--- Skiing holidays
— City breaks

1 The graph shows the popularity of three different types of holiday from 1990 to 2020 in millions of travellers. ....*T*....

2 City breaks increased gradually from 2 million travellers in 1990 to 3 million in 2010. ....

3 There was a slight increase in skiing holidays after 1990, then they remained stable for about 5 years. ....

4 From 2010 to 2020 it is predicted that there will be a sharp rise in the number of people who go on skiing holidays. ....

5 Beach holidays have decreased gradually from over 4 million to 3.5 million travellers. ....

6 From 2010 to 2020 there was a sharp drop in the number of people who went on skiing holidays. ....

2 **Look at the line graph below. Complete the sentences with the correct form of the verbs in brackets.**

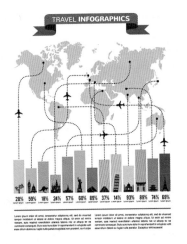

TRAVEL **INFOGRAPHICS**

Holiday costs for tourists 1990–2020 (in millions)

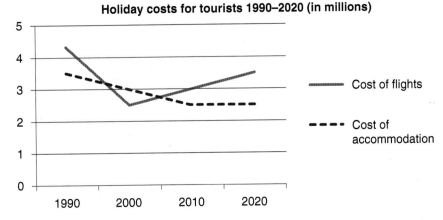

——— Cost of flights

- - - - Cost of accommodation

1 The line graph .... (show) the cost of holidays for tourists from 1990 to 2020.

2 Between 1990 and 2000 the cost of flights .... (drop) rapidly.

3 The cost of accommodation .... (go down) gradually for thirty years after 1990.

4 It is predicted that the cost of accommodation .... (stay) the same from 2010 to 2020.

3 **Look at the line graph below. Complete the text with the correct form of the verbs in brackets and the correct prepositions.**

Number of tourists per month in summer, 2009 (in thousands)

——— Japan

- - - Thailand

••••• Singapore

June   July   August   September

The graph (**1**) .... (show) how many tourists (**2**) ....
(visit) three countries in the summer of 2009. Most tourists (**3**) ....
(go) to Singapore (**4**) .... June and September. The number
(**5**) .... (fluctuate) between 3 and 4.5 thousand. Fewer tourists
(**6**) .... (travel) to Japan and Thailand. The number of people who
visited Thailand (**7**) .... (drop) gradually from 2.5 thousand to about
1.8 from June to August and then (**8**) .... (rise) to 3 thousand
(**9**) .... September. We can (**10**) .... (see) that the trend
for Japan (**11**) .... (be) similar. There was a sharp drop in tourists from
June to July. The number (**12**) .... (remain) stable between mid-July
and mid-August and then (**13**) .... (increase) steadily after that.

Practice for the test

Task 1

You should spend about 20 minutes on this task.

The line graph below shows the percentage of tourists to Scotland who visited four different attractions in Edinburgh. Summarize the information by selecting and reporting the main features, and make comparisons where relevant.

Write at least 150 words.

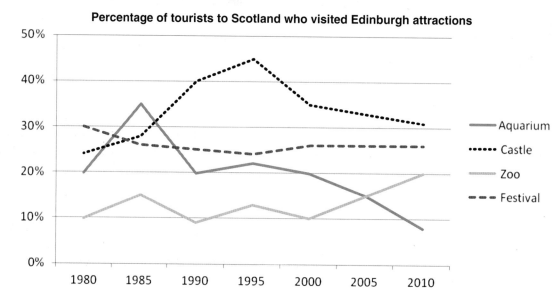

Percentage of tourists to Scotland who visited Edinburgh attractions

Listening

completing forms and notes • answering multiple-choice questions

Exam tip

Before you listen, look at the information you have been given to complete. Predicting the kind of answers you need will help you to focus on what you are going to hear.

see **GRAMMAR** page 154 and more **PRACTICE** online

Develop your exam skills

info

In Section 1 of the Listening test you will hear two people talking in an everyday or social situation. You may have to complete notes or a form with details of names, addresses, times or dates. You will need to listen carefully for spellings and numbers.

74 **1** You will hear a conversation between two friends planning a visit. Predict the kind of information you think you have to listen for (numbers, letters, time, name, etc.). Then listen and complete the notes.

> Sam arrives at: (1) .... on: (2) ....
>
> Airline/Flight number: (3) ....

75 **2** Look at the numbers below both in figures and written form. Listen and circle the numbers you hear. Then match them with their written forms.

> 18   13   15   30   80   40   14   50
>
> fifteen   thirteen   eighteen   fourteen   fifty   forty   eighty   thirty

76 **3** You will now hear numbers in short sentences. Write down the numbers you hear.

1 .... 2 .... 3 .... 4 .... 5 ....

77/78 **4** You will hear two conversations that include names. Choose the correct letter a, b or c for each conversation.

1 a McKeon   b McEwan   c MacKeon

2 a Westborne   b Westerborne   c Westbourne

Exam tip

You will be expected to know the spellings of common words and names. Any unusual names will be spelt out for you. An answer spelt wrongly will be marked incorrect, so get plenty of practice before the exam.

79 **5** You will hear a telephone conversation in which Sam is booking a taxi. First look at the form and think about the kind of information you will need. Then listen and complete the form.

PLEASE USE BLOCK CAPITALS	
NAME OF PASSENGER:	SAM WILLIAMS
PICK-UP DATE AND TIME:	WED 6TH JULY (1) ....
PICK-UP POINT NO. & STREET: TOWN: POSTCODE:	(2) .... WILLOWSIDE BANK (3) .... (4) ....
MOBILE NUMBER:	(5) 07789 ....
DESTINATION:	HEATHROW – TERMINAL 5

6 You will hear a conversation between a flight attendant and a passenger arriving in the UK. Complete the form.

Family name LIU .... First name **(1)** ....

Sex

☐ M ☑ F

Town and country of birth SHENZHEN CHINA ....

Nationality CHINESE ....

Contact address in UK **(3)** ....

Date of birth

(2) | D | D | M | M | Y | Y | Y | Y |

Occupation STUDENT ....

Exam tip

When you complete a form, it is important to keep to the required number of words for each answer. You will be told how many words to use, e.g. NO MORE THAN TWO WORDS AND/ OR A NUMBER. If you write too many words, your answer will be marked incorrect.

A hyphenated word counts as one word, e.g. *mother-in-law*. A number can be written in letters or numbers, e.g. *twelve* or *12*; either way, it counts as one word.

Exam tip

During the exam, listen very carefully and don't presume the first information you hear is always correct. Sometimes the speaker can change his/her mind and correct the information given.

Practice for the test

Section 1

 Questions 1–7

You will hear a telephone conversation between a hotel receptionist and a caller making a reservation. Complete the form below. Write **NO MORE THAN THREE WORDS AND/OR A NUMBER** for each answer.

Number of nights	...................................1..........................
Type of room: *(circle one)*	**(1)** Single / Double – twin beds / Double – king-sized bed
Name	**(2)** ....
Home address	**(3)** .... Avenue, Cambridge
Postcode	**(4)** ....
Transport	**(5)** ....
Meals	**(6)** ....
Date of arrival	**(7)** ....

 Questions 8–10

Now listen to the next part of the conversation and choose the correct letter, **a, b or c.**

8 *The customer's mobile phone number is*
  a 07976 122577.
  b 07961 122577.
  c 07961 121597.

9 *The customer would also like to*
  a receive tourist information.
  b make a restaurant booking.
  c book tickets for the theatre.

10 *He leaves a message for*
  a Mr Alami.
  b Mr El Fassi.
  c Mr Alaoui.

Now listen again to check your answers before you look at the answer key.

Reading

Get READY for class!
Remember to do your preparation before class.
online • workbook

Develop your exam skills

> In the exam, you may be asked to demonstrate that you understand the points of view expressed in a text. You will be given a list of statements, each of which represents an opinion. You have to read the text to find out if the writer expresses these opinions or not. If the writer shares the opinion in the statement, your answer will be YES. If the writer contradicts the statement, your answer will be NO. If it is impossible to know from the text what the writer's opinion about that subject is, your answer will be NOT GIVEN. The information in the text will be in the same order as the list of statements.

1 Read the following statements. Write (F) for fact and (O) for opinion; an opinion does not have to be based on fact or knowledge and we cannot prove it right or wrong.

1 The distance between Birmingham and Cheltenham is about 40 miles.

   ....

2 There are currently two areas with roadworks between Birmingham and Cheltenham. ....

3 Cheltenham has music, literature and horseracing festivals, a historic promenade and award-winning gardens. ....

4 Cheltenham is well worth a visit. ....

5 Birmingham is sometimes compared to Venice because of its many canals.

   ....

6 You can't get from Birmingham to Cheltenham in less than half an hour unless you break the speed limit. ....

7 Frankley service station, on the M5 near Birmingham, has shops that provide good value for money. ....

2 Read the three texts and the statements that follow. Write YES if the opinion is expressed in the text (= the writer agrees) and NO if the writer disagrees.

Britain never used to have armed police, but when major events are being held, such as the 2012 London Olympics, there is a visible presence of armed police in train stations. Do people using public transport feel reassured when they see armed police? Possibly. But most of them, especially visitors to the UK, may feel that there is something to worry about, especially as they would expect British police not to be armed. And if we think about it, the police, armed or not, cannot protect us from bombs. But what the police can, and sometimes do, is make mistakes, and these are always worse when there are firearms involved. So in the end, arming police may do more harm than good.

1 Most travellers feel protected when they see armed police in train stations. NO

2 Even police with guns cannot protect us from bombs. ....

3 The police might shoot somebody by accident. ....

4 It is better not to have armed police in Britain. ....

Instead of complaining about roadworks, the cost of petrol, the price of cars, etc., we need to think about other options. And I don't mean car sharing or building more motorways.

I say we try to save our environment by campaigning for better bus and train networks and for different types of transport, such as trams.

5 We should complain about car-related problems. ....

6 The environment is not really in danger. ....

7 Public transport needs to be improved. ....

The rise in fuel prices is a very worrying trend. Here are just some examples of the consequences. Elderly people cannot afford to heat their houses, people lose their jobs because they can no longer afford to commute to work, or because they are made redundant from their jobs in transport-based businesses such as airlines. Self-employed people often rely on their own transport for work, e.g. delivery people, florists and taxi drivers, so they may be forced to close their business.

The prices of some food and raw materials also increase as a direct result of the cost of oil, e.g. the prices of beef and cotton. Against all of that, there is one possible advantage: car manufacturers are employing more people to design fuel-efficient cars, which will benefit the environment. But surely this is not enough. What we need is international cooperation and political goodwill to reduce fuel prices and / or financially support those who are being affected.

8 We need to be concerned about the increase in the price of fuel. ....

9 There are more problems caused by increasing fuel prices than the ones mentioned in the passage. ....

10 The price of beef is closely related to the price of oil. ....

11 The rise of fuel prices is not a problem as the environment benefits from it. ....

12 If we cannot lower the price of fuel, we need more money so people can cope with it. ....

Exam tip

To help you determine if something is NOT GIVEN, look for synonyms and paraphrases. If none appear, the answer will probably be NOT GIVEN. But even if you do find paraphrases, be careful: it may be that the topic is mentioned but not in relation to the statement.

3 Re-read the three texts and the statements in Exercise 2. Identify synonyms and paraphrases that were used in the statements. For each statement in Exercise 2, underline the word(s) in the text that helped you.

4 Re-read the third text in Exercise 2. Are the following opinions in the text (✓) or are they NOT GIVEN?

1 Old people may die because they cannot keep warm. ....

2 There is more unemployment when fuel prices rise. ....

3 People who deliver goods may use their personal vehicles to do this. ....

4 The price of corn and corn-based foods are related to the price of oil. ....

5 There already exist some fuel-efficient cars. ....

6 Politicians are not working hard enough now to solve fuel price problems. ....

Practice for the test

Questions 1–12

Read the following text. Do the statements agree with the writer's views? Write:

YES if the statement agrees with the views of the writer

NO if the statement contradicts what the writer thinks

NOT GIVEN if it is impossible to know what the writer's point of view is

1 Another name for the East-West trading route is Silk Road. ....

2 Zhang Qian is admired by Chinese schoolchildren. ....

3 Zhang Qian was a Chinese adventurer. ....

4 At least one German used the Silk Road in the 19th century. ....

5 Silk was the main material to be traded on this route. ....

6 The Silk Road carried natural and man-made materials, as well as animals. ....

7 We know that Zhang Qian was the first person to use the Silk Road. ....

8 The Romans may well have used the Silk Road. ....

9 Reports of a 'stone tower' prove that the Romans used the Silk Road. ....

10 Kashgar is a welcoming city. ....

11 People who go into the Taklaman desert never come back out. ....

12 The difficult journey from the west probably stopped travellers getting to China. ....

Schoolchildren in China learn that the opening of the East-West trading route popularly known as the Silk Road occurred in 139 BC, when Zhang Qian, the Chinese ambassador-adventurer, travelled westward across the Pamirs, a mountain range in Central Asia. He was the first known Chinese person to do so. The term 'Silk Road' was actually first used late in the nineteenth century. Silk was not the only material that passed along these routes. Other goods included ceramics, glass, precious gems and livestock.

However, there are reasons to think that these roads were being used centuries earlier than Zhang's expedition. In Roman times, Pliny the Elder reported a 'stone tower', which he said existed on the Pamir Plateau where goods had been traditionally exchanged between traders from the East and the West. In the early second century, Maës Titianus, an ancient Roman-Macedonian traveller, reported reaching this famous Stone Tower. According to one theory, it was at Tashkurgan in the Pamirs ('Tashkurgan' means 'stone tower' in the Uyghur language). Scholars today, however, believe that its location was probably somewhere in the Alay Valley. Whatever the truth may be, it seems likely that some form of trade was taking place in this region millennia before more formal recorded trade took place.

On the other hand, it is difficult to believe that people in those times were able to travel such huge distances. Travelling from West to East, the trader first had to cross the Pamir Plateau, through the 20,000-foot-high mountains. If the weather in the mountains was kind, the eastward bound traveller would then finally arrive at the city of Kashgar, a logical place for trade and rest, where they could exchange horses or camels and then start on the return journey back over the mountains before the winter snows.

It is unlikely that in these earlier times traders or travellers would have continued further eastwards from Kashgar, as they would have had to go round the Taklamakan Desert. Going through it may not have been an option: the name literally means 'Go in and you won't come out'. Beyond this desert, there still would have remained eight hundred miles of a dangerous journey before they would have found the first signs of Chinese civilization.

Adapted from The Moon over Matsushima – Insights into Mugwort and Moxa, by Merlin Young (Godiva Press).

Unit 10

Health

Listening

completing notes • completing tables and flow charts • matching information

Get READY for class!

Remember to do your preparation before class.

online • workbook

Exam tip

When you complete notes about the stages in a process, for example in a flow chart, listen carefully for words that indicate the order of the different parts of the procedure, such as *first, then, after that* and *at the end*.

Develop your exam skills

info

In Section 2 of the Listening test you will hear one person talking about a topic of general interest. You may have to complete notes, a table or a flow chart describing a process.

🎧 83 **1** **You will hear a chef giving her students a list of ingredients for a regional dish. Match the ingredients with the quantities. You will not use them all.**

1 chicken **2** rice **3** onions **4** tomatoes **5** green peppers **6** cooking oil

 e ....

a 450 g **b** 4 kilos **c** ¾ kilo **d** 500 g **e** 2 kilos **f** 15 ml **g** 50 ml **h** ¼ kilo

🎧 84 **2** **You will hear how to cook pancakes on a TV programme called Campus Cook-in. Listen to the recording and put the photos in the correct order.**

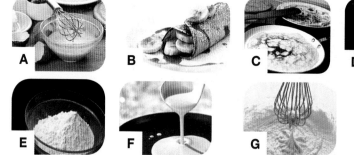

A **B** **C** **D**

E **F** **G**

🎧 85 **3** **You will hear someone describe how to cook a dessert. Read the instructions and think about which words go in the gaps. Then listen and complete the flow chart. Write NO MORE THAN FOUR WORDS for each answer.**

Peel and (1) .... → Cook (2) .... → Mix (3) .... → Put in bottom of (4) ....

Bake for (8) .... ← Put mixture (7) .... ← Add (6) .... ← Rub (5) ....

4 You will hear a student representative talking about traditional English meals. Read the notes below. Then listen and complete the notes. Write **NO MORE THAN TWO WORDS OR A NUMBER** for each answer.

Very popular dish : Fish and chips: fried in (1) .... — not (2) ....

Popular esp. (3) ....

Another traditional meal: Sunday lunch (4) .... meat , with (5) ....

Traditionally eaten (6) ....

Practice for the test

Section 2

Questions 1–4

 You will hear a talk on nutrition. Complete the notes. Write **NO MORE THAN TWO WORDS** for each answer.

Topic: Healthy eating

- definition
- reasons why people don't
  (1) ....
- ideas for (2) ....

Healthy eating is:

- balanced diet
- eating the (3) ....

Note: balanced diet incl. meat, veg, fruit, cereals & (4) ....

 #### Questions 5–7

Now you will hear the next part of the recording. Choose **THREE** letters, a–h. Give three reasons why many people have an unhealthy diet.

a It is cheaper to buy packet food.
b People do not know how to eat healthily.
c It is cheaper to buy fast food.
d They prefer fast food.

e They do not like packet food.
f It is quicker to buy fast food.
g They have to plan their meals.
h Schools teach children about a balanced diet.

5 ....   6 ....   7 ....

 #### Questions 8–10

Now listen to the last part of the recording and complete the table. Write **NO MORE THAN ONE WORD** for each answer.

Group responsible:		
(8)	(9)	(10) ....
Limit advertising for unhealthy food	Stop selling unhealthy snacks and drinks	Make sure children eat a balanced diet
Educate the public about a healthy diet	Provide children with fresh and healthy options	

Speaking

giving explanations • pronunciation: contractions • *should / shouldn't* • understanding different types of questions

Develop your exam skills

 Part 1 tests your ability to answer different questions about your life. Part 3 tests your ability to give your opinion on different topics.

1 **Read the Part 1 questions and answers below. For each question, choose the relevant answer, a or b.**

1 Do you enjoy watching sports?

  a Yes, I enjoy watching sports. I like watching football and golf.

  b Yes, I enjoy sports. I play football every week and I think sport is good for you.

2 Do you work or are you a student?

  a I'm a student and I'm studying English. I'm in my first year at university.

  b I started studying English when I was at school. It was my favourite subject.

3 When do you see your friends and family?

  a Every day. I'm living with my parents and I see my friends at college every day.

  b Every day. I'm living with my parents and I visit my grandparents every weekend.

4 What do you like doing in your free time?

  a I don't have lots of hobbies because I work long hours.

  b I like meeting friends and relaxing. I really enjoy shopping and going to the cinema.

Exam tip

Remember to only talk about relevant points or information in your answer.

2 **Read the questions in Exercise 1 again. Record your answers. Then listen and assess your answers. Are they relevant to the question?**

 3 **Listen to three Part 3 questions and write 1, 2 or 3 next to each choice. Are they asking you to:**

  a give your opinion on an issue? ....

  b compare the past to the present? ....

  c make a suggestion? ....

Exam tip

Pay attention to the examiner's questions. Understand the type of question you have to answer: opinion, comparison or suggestion.

 4 **Read the three answers below to the questions you heard in Exercise 3. Underline any words and phrases you think will help understand what kind of answers these are, e.g. *I think, we should, the past*. Then listen and check.**

  a Definitely. I think relaxing is a very important part of being healthy. We're always busy. We're travelling to work or college, we're meeting friends, we're doing homework. So in my opinion, I think it's important to slow down and relax. It's good for our bodies and our minds.

  b That's a difficult question. Let me see. Unfortunately, in my country, young people like playing computer games and they usually like eating junk food. We should encourage them to play games outdoors. For example, they could go to the beach and do water sports. We should encourage them to learn about food and cook some healthy food with their families.

  c That's interesting. I think it's important to play sports. There are lots of different sports now, and you can learn a new sport wherever you live, not like the past. Sports people earn a good salary. I think it's a good job. I'd like to be a professional golfer. But there are some boring sports. For example, I don't like watching motor racing.

5 Read the answers again and complete the table below.

	Answer a	Answer b	Answer c
1 Is the answer relevant to the question?			
2 What is the opinion, comparison or suggestion?			

see GRAMMAR page 158 and more PRACTICE online

 6 Listen to the Part 3 questions in Exercise 3 again and record your answers. Then listen to your answers and assess each one.

- Is your answer relevant to the question?
- What is your opinion, comparison and suggestion?

 7 You will hear three Part 3 questions. Decide what the question is asking for (opinion, comparison or suggestion). Work with a partner and give your answers.

Practice for the test

Part 1

 1 Listen to five Part 1 questions. Record your answer to each question.

Part 2

Exam tip

Remember to use the present simple to talk about things you like doing in your life.

2 Read the Part 2 task card below. Plan your answer. You have one minute for this in the exam. Then record your answer. You have one to two minutes for this.

> **Describe an activity you like doing to keep healthy.**
>
> You should say:
>
> what it is
> when and where you do it
> how it keeps you healthy
>
> and explain why you like doing it.

3 Answer the questions below to complete Part 2. Record your answer.

1 Do your family like doing this activity?
2 Would you like to spend more time on this activity?

Part 3

 4 Listen to four Part 3 questions. Answer the questions and record your answers.

Reading

Answering short-answer questions

Exam tip

To keep to the maximum number of words, it can help to change a word form. Use a noun as an adjective, e.g. *the documents about the house → the house documents*, or omit a verb, e.g. *there is a variety of reasons → various reasons*.

Develop your exam skills

> **info**
>
> In the exam, you may have to look for facts in a passage and give short answers to questions. You will be told how many words to use in the answers. A number can be written either as a word, e.g. *four*, or as a number, e.g. *4*, and counts as one word. A word with a hyphen, e.g. *mother-in-law*, counts as one word. You will not be required to use contractions.

1 The following instructions were given in an IELTS Reading test: 'Using NO MORE THAN FOUR WORDS for each, answer the following questions'. Look at the students' answers in the table and shorten them if necessary.

Question	Students' answers	Short answer
1 What were his parents afraid of?	there was a possibility that he would have problems with his health (12 words)	*his possible health problems* (4 words)
2 When did they first find out there was a problem?	when doctors did a medical examination during the mother's pregnancy	
3 How does his illness affect him?	at the moment he is not affected by it at all but he needs to take medication	
4 What will happen in the future?	nobody knows that yet	

2 Answer these questions in **NO MORE THAN THREE WORDS.**

1 What do you think is the best way to lose weight? ....

2 How do you feel about football? ....

3 What do you enjoy doing in your free time? ....

4 Why is exercise important? ....

3 Read this list of possible ways to help answer questions. Delete two activities that would NOT help you answer questions 1–3. Explain your reasons.

- reading the questions slowly before reading the text
- underlining the key words in the questions
- reading the text before reading the questions
- underlining the key words in the text
- scanning (moving your eyes down over the text to find information you are looking for, without reading the text word for word)

1 Why do some people accept pain as a part of life?

2 What did Blaxter want to find out about?

3 What does the text say about how older people define health?

4 Re-read the questions in Exercise 3 and scan the text below. Underline the key words in the questions. Answer the questions using NO MORE THAN THREE WORDS for each answer.

1 .... 3 ....

2 ....

Illness is defined in a variety of ways, which depend on a number of factors. One of these factors is age differences. Older people tend to accept as 'normal' a range of pains and physical limitations which younger people would define as symptoms of some illness or disability. As we age, we gradually redefine health and accept greater levels of physical discomfort. In Blaxter's national survey of health definitions (1990), she found that young people tend to define health in terms of physical fitness, but gradually, as people age, health comes to be defined more in terms of being able to cope with everyday tasks. She found examples of older people with really serious arthritis who nevertheless defined themselves as healthy, as they were still able to carry out a limited range of routine activities.

Glossary

arthritis: a medical condition in which the joints (such as the knees or fingers) in someone's body are painful

Practice for the test

info

Just as with multiple-choice questions, short-answer questions are normally in the same order as the information in the text. Sometimes in short-answer tasks, the instructions will ask you to use words taken directly from the text.

Questions 1–10

Using NO MORE THAN FOUR WORDS for each, answer the following questions.

1 In what ways do our bodies physically differ?

....

2 Why do our bodies differ physically?

....

3 What types of jobs are poor people likely to have?

....

4 What aspects of poor people's living environments are not good?

....

5 What influences how groups of people value bodies?

....

6 What have wealthy cultures changed their opinion about?

....

7 In the past, what part of the body could indicate that people were rich?

....

8 According to sociologists, in what ways should we think about the body?

....

9 Which two physical factors contribute to whether people are obese or not?

....

10 What does society say that being obese is?

....

The body

The concept of 'the body' is closely related to the ideas of 'illness' and 'health'.

All of us exist in 'bodies' of different shapes, heights, colours and physical abilities. The main reasons for the differences are genetic, and the fact that people's bodies change as they age. However, a huge range of research indicates that there are social factors too.

Poorer people are more likely to eat 'unhealthy' foods, to smoke cigarettes and to be employed in repetitive, physically difficult work, or the opposite: boring, inactive employment.

Moreover, their housing conditions and neighbourhoods tend to be worse. All of these factors impact upon the condition of a person's health: the physical shapes of bodies are strongly influenced by social factors.

These social factors are also closely linked to emotional wellbeing. People with low or no incomes are more likely to have mental health problems. It is not clear, however, whether poverty causes mental illness, or whether it is the other way around. For example, certain people with mental health issues may be at risk of becoming homeless, just as a person who is homeless may have an increased risk of illnesses such as depression.

There are other types of social factors too. Bodies are young or old, short or tall, big or small, weak or strong. Whether these judgments matter and whether they are positive or negative depends on the cultural and historical context. The culture and media of different societies promote very different valuations of body shapes. What is considered as attractive or ugly, normal or abnormal varies enormously. Currently, for example, in rich societies the ideal of slimness is highly valued, but historically this was different. In most societies the ideal body shape for a woman was a 'full figure' with a noticeable belly, while in middle-aged men, a large stomach indicated that they were financially successful in life. In many traditional African and Pacific island cultures, for example, a large body shape was a sign of success and a shape to be aimed at.

It is easy for people to feel undervalued because of factors they have no power to change, for example, their age and height. Equally, they can feel pressured into making changes to their appearance – when it is possible to make such changes – which in extreme cases can lead to obsessions with weight loss and fitness regimes.

Sociologists, then, are suggesting that we should not just view bodies and minds in biological terms, but also in social terms. The physical body and what we seek to do with it change over time. This has important implications for medicine and ideas of health. Thus, the idea of people being 'obese' is physically related to large amounts of processed food, together with lack of exercise, and is therefore a medical issue. However, it has also become a mental health issue and social problem as a result of people coming to define this particular body shape as 'wrong' and unhealthy.

Writing

see **GRAMMAR**
page 157 and more
PRACTICE online

Exam tip

Only use *will / would*
in the result clause
of a conditional
sentence if you are
stating a well-known
fact. In an essay, it is
usually better to use
indefinite language
such as *may / can
/ could / might* to
express opinions or
possible, rather than
definite, results.

*If you smoke, you will
become very ill.* ✗

*If you smoke, you
might / may become
very ill.* ✓

Develop your exam skills

> **info**
>
> For Task 2 you might need to write about the causes and effects of a
> problem or issue. Use conditional sentences and linking words such as
> *because, so, therefore* and *as a result (of)* to describe causes and effects
> clearly.

1 **Read the essay paragraph below. Underline the cause and effect sentences.
Then label each cause (C) and each effect (E). An example has been done
for you.**

*A country that has free healthcare has a healthier population. To what extent do you
agree or disagree?*

Healthcare should be free in every country because it helps improve the health
of the population. Some things, such as computers, cars or holidays are luxuries
which people should pay for themselves, but healthcare is a necessity not a luxury.
(C) <u>If people do not have access to free healthcare,</u> (E) <u>minor health problems may
become much worse</u>. There is also a second important issue to take into account.
If poor people have to pay for healthcare, they might not visit the doctor when they
are ill. If healthcare becomes more expensive, there may be some negative effects in
the future. For example, if only rich people can afford healthcare, they may be much
healthier and may live longer than poor people. The result of this could be an unequal
and divided society.

2 **Read another paragraph from the essay in Exercise 1. Complete the
paragraph using the phrases below.**

> if people have unhealthy lifestyles   they should pay for it themselves
> free healthcare might not do them much good

However, free healthcare does not always result in a healthy population.
For example, if people choose to have an unhealthy lifestyle,
(**1**) .... Some people believe that
(**2**) ...., they should not receive free
healthcare. In addition, healthcare comes in many forms and some of these forms
may not be essential. Most people think that if people want cosmetic surgery simply
to improve their appearance, (**3**) ....
However, doctors think that there may be good medical reasons for some forms of
cosmetic surgery.

3 Look at different structures for describing causes and effects on page 104. Notice the order of the causes and effects and the words in green.

        effect   *cause*
*People can become fat **because** they eat too much bad food.*

            cause   *effect*
***Because** people eat too much bad food, they can become fat.*

Now complete the sentences for the essay using the phrases below, marking each cause (C) and each effect (E).

Obesity is a common problem in many societies. What are the main causes of obesity and what are the effects?

> their parents do not teach them
> ~~they do not eat enough vegetables~~
> aren't active enough.
>
> people do not shop for fresh food.
> they do not get enough exercise.
> they tax them heavily.

1 People have become accustomed to junk food *C*_____, **so** *they do not eat enough vegetables* _____ *E* .

2 **Because** young children spend too much time watching television ...., ...

3 Many people have office jobs which do not involve any physical activity ....
As a result, they ....

4 **Because**
....
...., children do not know how to cook for themselves ....

5 **Due to** the availability of cheap fast food, ...,
....
....

6 Governments earn a lot of money from fast-food companies .... **because**
....

4 Read the text below. Correct four more mistakes with linking words.

Exercise is an important part of a healthy life. If people don't exercise, they will become unhealthy. Nowadays, many people don't get enough exercise ~~due to~~ *because* they have jobs where they sit down all day. Additionally, life is easier. In the old days, people had to wash clothes by hand or make their own bread. Result, they were more active in their lives. Also, people didn't have cars in the old days, because they had to walk everywhere. This meant that people were active in their daily life. Now, due cars and machines which make life easier, people don't do as much. In result, they have become more unfit.

5 Read the essay title and the cause and effect sentences in the table. Match causes to effects. Then write the headings 'Causes' and 'Effects' in the correct places.

Modern technology is a threat to the health of people all over the world.

What are the main effects of modern technology on our health?

....	....
1 Children spend too much time sitting playing video games.	a People can develop wrist problems or back pain.
2 Using social media is a common hobby for many people nowadays.	b They cannot hear cars coming and may get run over.
3 Ready meals are easy to buy.	c They do not move enough so they become overweight.
4 Office jobs involve too much time working with computers.	d People don't cook fresh food any more.
5 People in the street listen to music through headphones.	e Face-to-face activities such as sports are less popular.

6 Write a paragraph for the essay in Exercise 5 using some of the causes and effects in the table. Write approximately 60–80 words. Start your paragraph like this:

Many health problems today may be caused by modern technology. For example,

....
....
....
....
....
....
....
....
....

Exam tip

A good way of building your argument is to write the topic sentence of a paragraph and then add a cause and effect sentence to explain it:

An inactive lifestyle is bad for people. If people don't exercise and move around, they may become ill.

Practice for the test

Task 2

You should spend about 40 minutes on this task.
Write about the following topic:

Governments should introduce healthcare which prevents illness rather than cures it.

How far do you agree with this statement?

Give reasons for your answer and include any relevant examples from your own knowledge or experience.

Write at least 250 words.

Taking responsibility

Reading

Matching sentence endings

Get READY **for class!**

Remember to do your preparation before class.

online • workbook

Exam tip

Try to predict how each sentence will end before looking at the list of endings.

Exam tip

Focusing on the key words in the instructions and looking for synonyms and paraphrasing in the text will help you write sentences with the correct information and grammar. Look for the key words in the sentence beginnings, not the endings: don't waste time reading through all the endings in detail.

Develop your exam skills

info

In the exam, you may be given a number of incomplete sentences. You will need to complete them by choosing from a list of options. They will be in the order of the text. There will be more options than you need.

1 **Read the following sentence beginnings. Try to predict what type of word comes next: verb, noun, adjective, adverb or preposition.**

1 The African Charter on the rights and welfare of the ....

2 The name was chosen ....

3 This Children's Charter ....

4 It covers the economic, social, political and cultural ....

2 **Read the following sentence endings. Match them to the sentence beginnings in Exercise 1.**

a ... by a national council. ....

b ... child has existed for many decades. ....

c ... rights of African children. ....

d ... was written in 1990. ....

3 **The following text has been divided into four parts. Skim-read the first paragraph of each part to identify what the complete text is about. Then choose the best sentence endings for 1–3 from the three options.**

Human rights are ideas about what everyone is entitled to. Basic human rights include the right to life, and the right to food and clean drinking water. Others include the right to vote and to freedom of expression. In the UK, most people have their basic human rights met most of the time. However, in some countries people's freedoms may be limited. Also, in the UK, there are still areas of human rights that some people believe could be improved, such as the rights of people with disabilities.

The modern idea of human rights was developed after the Second World War, during which many people's rights were violated. On a large scale, these human rights abuses are known as war crimes. As a result, the United Nations (UN) was formed to provide a place for nations to resolve conflicts peacefully. It was set up by the Universal Declaration of Human Rights (UDHR), which consisted of 30 articles describing the basic rights of every person, and was signed in 1948 by 48 countries.

1 *Human rights*

   a are about having everything you need and want.

   b apply especially to people with disabilities.

   c are about rights and also about freedoms.

2 *Human rights*

   a did not exist before the Second World War.

   b are less important when there is a war.

   c are now an international issue.

The first section of the Universal Declaration states: 'All human beings are born free and equal in dignity and rights.'

Key rights relating to being 'born free' include freedom of speech and of movement, the right to a fair trial, and freedom from torture and from hunger.

Key rights relating to 'being equal' include a right to an education, and the right to be treated equally, without discrimination, in all areas of public life.

The Universal Declaration was designed as a safeguard to protect the human rights of people around the world.

3 *According to the Universal Declaration, it is a person's right to*

   a be accepted everywhere in public.   **b** receive an education   **c** have equal treatment.

A legal basis for human rights

The European Convention of Human Rights was drawn up in 1963, giving a legal framework for human rights in the UK and other European countries. Here, people can complain to the European Court of Human Rights (ECHR), based in Strasbourg, France. In 1998, the European Union (EU) decided to update the list of human rights, to take account of changes in society and technology. The result was the European Charter of Fundamental Rights (2000). This included some newer human rights:

- The right to a private life, including the right to privacy and to confidentiality of letters and emails.

- The right to a limit on working hours and to have an annual paid holiday.

- The right to respect the integrity of human beings, including a ban on financial gain from the human body. This includes the sale of human organs and the cloning of human beings.

- The right to data protection, which means that if a company holds data on you, you can ask where it got the information and what it is.

4 *The European Charter of Fundamental Rights*

   a resulted in social and technological changes.

   b included information about rights relating to new technology.

   c replaced older declarations of human rights.

People aged 17 and under

For children and young people there is The United Nation's Convention on the Rights of the Child (UNCRC), which covers economic, social, cultural and political rights. The UK agreed to obey the rules of the convention in 1991, which means that every child in the UK, without exception, has certain rights that he or she is entitled to, more than 40 in total. Here are some examples:

- The right to life, survival and development

- The right to have their views respected, and to have their best interests considered at all times

- The right to a name and nationality, freedom of expression, and access to information concerning them

- The right to education, leisure, culture and the arts

5 *If you are under 18,*

   a you should have economic, cultural and other rights.

   b you should obey the rules of the 1991 convention.

   c you have over 40 rights.

Practice for the test

Questions 1–5

Complete each sentence with the correct ending A–I.

1 Students' views are likely to be taken seriously if there are ....

2 Rules relating to uniform are most likely to be discussed at ....

3 Year councils may get involved in ....

4 In the Year 8 council that is mentioned, teachers make sure that students are ....

5 Those in power are ....

A bullying and fundraising.	**F** representative from some year groups.
B more likely to bully others.	**G** school councils and peer mentoring.
C not always the best listeners.	**H** school councils.
D not left on their own.	**I** teachers and parents of older students.
E organizing events.	

Participating in the school community

It is important that students' feelings, opinions and suggestions are listened to, taken into account, and that the right action is taken. There are a number of ways that this can be achieved, i.e. school councils and peer mentoring.

School councils

Most schools have a school council, which exists to let the teachers and head teacher know what students' opinions are on a range of school issues. This usually consists of two or three elected representatives from each year group. A school council might meet once or twice a month to discuss issues such as the dress code, charity fundraising and bullying.

Year councils

School councils are sometimes dominated by older students, so some schools have year councils. The aim of these is to give students the opportunity to express opinions on matters of importance to their year group. The following is an example of the rules relating to a school's council for Year 8.

1 The council's purpose is to act as a forum for discussion of school issues relevant to Year 8, and to let the teachers and head teacher know what student opinion is on these issues. The council will also take responsibility for cooperating with year staff in the organization of one social event per term for Year 8.

2 Membership of the council will consist of three representatives from each class, elected on a termly basis.

3 Meetings will be held once a fortnight. The council members will elect a chair to control the meetings and a secretary who will be responsible for circulating the agenda for each meeting and taking and circulating minutes of meetings.

4 The class representatives will be responsible for giving a report of the council's meetings to their class.

5 The Year 8 council will elect two of its members to the school council, with responsibility for raising issues on behalf of Year 8 students at school council meetings.

6 The chair, secretary and school council representatives will be responsible for taking up matters raised at council meetings with the year head and other teachers, and for reporting back on such matters to the Year 8 council.

7 The head of year will attend all council meetings as an observer and both the head of the year and the other year staff will be available to offer support and advice to council members and to assist in the settlement of disputes.

Peer mentoring

There are other ways in which students' voices can be heard. One of the most popular schemes involves peer mentoring. Those who express an interest receive training to become mentors so that they are better equipped to help others. This starts from primary school age, when the mentors may get involved in issues relating to conflict resolution. At secondary school and university, mentors deal with more varied issues, such as educational and health-related matters.

The underlying belief in schemes like these is that being heard by your peers can be more effective and helpful as fellow students may have more time and understanding than teachers or others in authority.

Writing

Develop your exam skills

For Task 2 you might need to write a problem and solution essay. For this essay you will need to think about and explain the problems of a situation or issue and consider and evaluate more than one possible solution.

There are two possible structures for a problem and solution essay:

1 Introduce the situation in the introduction

   Paragraph 1 = problem 1 + solution(s)

   Paragraph 2 = problem 2 + solution(s)

   Conclusion

2 Introduce the situation in the introduction

   Paragraph 1 = all problems

   Paragraph 2 = all solutions

   Conclusion

1 **Read the essay title and the list of problems and solutions below. Write P (problem) or S (solution) next to each idea. Explain the reasons for your choice.**

Many cities suffer from traffic-related problems. What problems does traffic cause in cities and what are the possible solutions?

1 The government should increase road tax. ....

2 People should use their cars less and public transport more. ....

3 Traffic jams create stress in people's lives. ....

4 The cost of travelling by bus or train needs to be cheaper. ....

5 There is a lot of air pollution in cities. ....

6 Public transport is too crowded. ....

7 Many accidents happen because there are so many cars on the roads. ....

8 If driving tests were more difficult, there would be fewer cars on the roads. ....

2 **Look at these ideas for the essay in Exercise 1. Match problems 1–4 to solutions a–d. Discuss the proposed solutions with a partner.**

Problems	Solutions
1 Traffic jams are caused by too many cars and lorries.	a People should pay to drive into cities during busy times such as mornings and evenings.
2 Public transport is expensive so people do not use it.	b The government could help reduce train and bus fares.
3 Air pollution caused by traffic has increased health problems.	c The number of vehicles allowed into city centres should be limited to reduce the amount of traffic.
4 Traffic problems in cities increase journey times to work and school.	d Environmentally-friendly cars should be cheaper.

see **GRAMMAR** page 158 and more **PRACTICE** online

3 Read this essay title and notes for four paragraphs below. Think about the best order for the four paragraphs for a structure 1 problem and solution essay. Put the notes in order, A–D.

Public transport is essential but problematic. Describe some of the problems connected to public transport and suggest some solutions.

1 problem 2: poor/slow service, e.g. too many stops/slow journeys, bad links between buses/trains, lack of public transport in countryside; solutions: fast lanes/routes for buses; coordinate bus/train timetables; cheaper fares for travellers in country ....

2 public transport essential — going to/from work, school, etc.; expensive — crowded; needs better planning, etc. Essay will describe problems/suggest possible solutions ....

3 problem 1: cost/high fares, people do not use public transport = more cars; solutions: reduce fares for some people, e.g. old/students; make driving and cost of cars/parking more expensive/tax more → public transport = cheaper ...
....

4 although challenges, solutions for these challenges; people must accept own responsibility; overall public transport is good thing; must be properly planned ...
....

4 Expand the notes into full sentences and write the four-paragraph essay in your notebook.

5 It is important to check your writing before handing in your paper to improve your score. Read the key areas where mistakes often occur below. Then underline six errors in the paragraph for this essay title and correct each error.

> *Singular / Plural: There are many <u>type</u> of transport.* type ✗ types ✓
>
> *Subject – verb agreement: Train fares <u>costs</u> too much money.* costs ✗ cost ✓
>
> *Incorrect part of speech: Traffic jams make people <u>anger</u>.* anger ✗ angry ✓

Air travel causes a variety of problems in the world and we should find alternative means of transport. Describe some of the problems caused by air travel and suggest some solutions.

First of all, air travel is a major causes of air pollution. The number of flights have increased dramatically over the last thirty years because people travel more for business, holidays and to visit friends and family. The pollution from air travel contributes significant to climate change. Some people feel that governments should spend most money on scientific research. They hope that scientists can find a different type of fuel which does not harming the environment as much. But people have to understand their own responsibility. They should find ways of travelling less as a reduce in the number of journeys would be the best solution.

6 Read the paragraph below. Match the underlined mistakes 1–6 to the categories a–f below. Then correct the mistakes.

6 **Read the paragraph below. Match the underlined mistakes 1–6 to the categories a–f below. Then correct the mistakes.**

Governments can do things to help, though. Air travel is too (1) <u>cheaper</u> so many people choose to fly rather than take other (2) <u>form</u> of transport. Governments should introduce new laws to increase the cost of flying. If airline companies decided (3) <u>charging</u> passengers more, people (4) <u>must</u> decide to use other forms of (5) <u>the</u> public transport such as trains or ships. Another solution could be to limit the number of flights in specific parts of the world or limit the number of flights each person (6) <u>take</u> in one year.

1 .....*e*.....   a   singular / plural ....
2 ....   b   infinitive with to / -ing form ....
3   c   incorrect article ....
4 ....   d   subject–verb agreement ....
5 ....   e   incorrect word form ....
6 ....   f   incorrect modal verb ....

Practice for the test

Task 2

You should spend about 40 minutes on this task.
Write about the following topic:

Motorways help people travel quickly and cover long distances but they also cause problems. What are the problems of motorways and what solutions are there?

Give reasons for your answer and include any relevant examples from your own knowledge or experience.

Write at least 250 words.

Speaking

describing feelings • pronunciation: giving emphasis • comparing • using the right tenses in answers

Get READY for class!

Remember to do your preparation before class.

online • workbook

Exam tip

Listen carefully to the examiner's question in Part 1. What is the grammatical tense? Answer with the best tense: past, present or future.

Develop your exam skills

info The Speaking test assesses your ability to use a range of relevant grammar to talk about the different IELTS topics.

1 **Read the Part 1 questions. Then choose the correct answer, a or b. What is the mistake in the other answer?**

1 Did you play any sports when you were a child?

  a Yes, I play lots of sports.

  b Yes, I played lots of sports.

2 What do you usually do on the Internet?

  a I use the Internet for chatting online and buying things.

  b I'm using the Internet for chatting online and buying things.

3 Are you a student or do you have a job?

  a I'm a student. I'm a student at university for two years.

  b I'm a student. I've been a student at university for two years.

 2 **You will hear five Part 1 questions. Choose the best beginning, a or b, for each answer.**

1 **a** It was in …		**b** It is in …	
2 **a** I was …		**b** I am …	
3 **a** I watched …		**b** I watch …	
4 **a** I studied …		**b** I'm studying …	
5 **a** I chose …		**b** I choose …	

 3 **Listen again to the questions in Exercise 2 and record your answers. Listen to your answers. Did you use the best tense? Use your answers in Exercise 2 to help.**

4 **Read the Part 2 task card. Which grammatical phrases and tenses below would be relevant in your answer?**

> present simple   past simple
> *there is/are   there was/were*
> *can/can't*   present continuous
> *have to   be going to   should*
> present perfect

Describe an enjoyable event you experienced when you were at school.

You should say:

when it happened
what was good about it
who was there

and what made it enjoyable.

 5 **You will hear a student answer to the Part 2 task card above. Listen and identify the grammatical phrases and tenses in the answer. How many are there?**

6 **Re-read the Part 2 task card in Exercise 4. Then plan what you will say in one minute. Record your answer. Try to talk for one to two minutes.**

7 Read the Part 3 question and answer below. Match the underlined phrases with the grammatical tenses and phrases 1–5.

> *In your opinion, what are the most important events at school?*

> *I think there are lots of important events. For example, the first day is important because you <u>meet</u> new friends. You <u>have to</u> remember lots of names and new things. Tests are important too. They're usually <u>more difficult</u> at a new school. Finally, your last day at school <u>is</u> important. Thankfully, there are no more tests and you<u>'re going</u> to start a new job or go to university. You<u>'re starting</u> a new life!*

1 obligation

2 present simple

3 comparing

4 present continuous

5 future

Exam tip

Listen to the grammatical tense in the Part 3 question and use this tense in the first part of your answer. Then use a range of grammatical phrases and tenses.

8 Read the question in Exercise 7 again. Record your answer. Which grammatical tenses and phrases did you use?

Practice for the test

Part 1

 1 Listen to five Part 1 questions. Record your answer to each question.

1 Do you come from a large family?

2 Did you have a favourite teacher at school?

3 Do you have any hobbies?

4 Describe your hometown.

5 What's your experience of travelling to other countries?

Part 2

 2 Listen to and read the Part 2 task card. Plan your answer. You have one minute for this in the exam. Then record your answer. You have one to two minutes for this in the exam.

> **Describe an important event in your life.**
>
> You should say:
>
> what the event was
> where and when it took place
> who was there
>
> and explain what made it important to you.

3 Answer the questions below to complete Part 2. Record your answer.

1 Do you think it's important to remember these types of event?

2 Do you think planned events are more enjoyable than events that aren't planned?

Part 3

 4 Listen to four Part 3 questions. Answer the questions and record your answers.

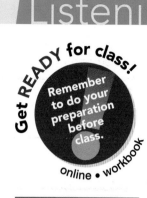

Get READY for class!

Remember to do your preparation before class.

online • workbook

Develop your exam skills

info

Remember that your answers must be grammatically correct and within the word count for sentence completion. Look for clues in the sentences you have to complete. For example, if the word before the gap is *an*, you should listen carefully for words beginning with a vowel (*a, e, i, o, u*).

 1 **You will hear a lecturer giving some students advice on how to balance their studies and their free time. Choose the correct completed sentences.**

1 **a** *So you'll have to do a lot more things for yourself,* like buying your own food, washing your clothes and managing your own money.

   b *So you'll have to do lots more things for yourself,* like buying your own food, washing your clothes and managing your own money.

2 **a** … at university you won't have as many hours *of class*

   b … at university you won't have as many hours *of classes*

3 **a** Actually, your university might even have a system for alerting you on your mobile *when your lecture is.*

   b Actually, your university might even have a system for alerting you on your mobile *when your lectures are.*

4 **a** One thing I will say, though, is that at the end of the year, *after your exam, you can really relax.*

   b One thing I will say, though, is that at the end of the year, *after your exams, you can really relax.*

 2 **You will hear a recording of a new employee describing the problems she has with time management. Listen and complete the sentences. Write NO MORE THAN THREE WORDS OR A NUMBER.**

1 In her previous job, the speaker worked from .... to ....

2 She now has to .... the office between 8.00 and 10.00 in the morning.

3 If she .... a lunch break, she can go home between 3.00 and 5.00 p.m.

4 .... she goes to the gym in the morning.

5 The children .... of school at 4.00.

3 **You are going to hear a talk about a project in Exercise 4. Before you listen, match the labels for a table, A–F, with alternatives, 1–6.**

Labels	Alternative expressions
A deadline	1 part
B finishing line	2 step in a process
C section	3 final date for completion
D start date	4 end of a race
E milestones	5 important achievements
F phase	6 beginning

Exam tip

While you are listening to the recording, remember to listen for the final *s* in verbs, possessives and plural nouns.

Exam tip

If you don't know the meaning of a word, don't worry. Focus on the words around it. They will give you an idea of the topic and the situation and will help you decide whether it is a key word. If it is important, try to guess the meaning from the situation. If it isn't, don't waste any time.

Exam tip

In this type of question, the information on the recording will be given in the same order as it is presented on the diagram, but may not be in the same words. Before you listen, read the answers and think about other words or expressions you might hear on the recording.

4 Listen to the market researcher describing how he plans a project. Write the headings in the table below. Choose FIVE and write the correct letters A–G.

> A Deadline   B Tasks   C Finishing line   D Section   E Start date
> F Milestones   G Completion of phase 1

(1)	(2)	(3)				(4)	(5) ....
Team meeting	23/01	15/02	18/03	25/04	30/06	15/08	15/09
Draft questionnaire							
Check questionnaire							
Complete survey							
Enter data on database							
Phase 1							
Write report							

Practice for the test

Questions 1–5

You will hear a human resource manager talking about her company's work-life balance policy. Complete the sentences. Write **NO MORE THAN TWO WORDS OR A NUMBER.**

1 The company is concerned about the physical .... health of the workers.

2 It aims to give employees a chance to create a balance between their work and .... lives.

3 Some parents need to work .... hours so they can look after their children.

4 A lot of parents work part time and others work ....

5 Women who have had a baby can take .... off work before they come back to the office.

Questions 6–8

Listen to the next part of the recording and label the pie chart. Write **NO MORE THAN THREE WORDS OR A NUMBER.**

Working pattern preferences

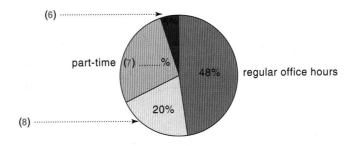

Questions 9–10

Listen to the last part of the recording and complete the notes. Write **NO MORE THAN THREE WORDS OR A NUMBER.**

Sally has **(9)** .... Leaves them at nursery before 8.00 a.m. Collects them from **(10)** .... house in the afternoon. Finishes her work at home.

Unit 12

Money

completing notes • answering matching questions • answering short-answer questions

Get READY for class!

Remember to do your preparation before class.

online • workbook

Exam tip

Listen carefully for words that tell you about the structure of the talk, for example, *first, next, now, finally.*

Exam tip

Before you answer multiple-choice questions, check that you know how many correct answers there are. In some cases, you have to choose *one* correct answer out of *three* possible options. In other questions you can choose *two* correct answers out of *five* options or *three* correct answers out of *seven* options.

Develop your exam skills

🎧 106 **1** These notes are from a talk on shopping habits. Complete the gaps with what you expect to hear. Then listen and check.

Who does the shopping?
— In the UK (1) .... % food bought by women.
— In some countries (2) .... % men do grocery shopping.
— Habits changing — US (3) .... of men shop for food.
Where do people shop?
— In cities (4)
— In country (5) .... and (6)

🎧 107 **2** You will hear a lecture about shopping habits. Underline the THREE statements you *think* are correct. Then listen and choose the THREE correct statements.

What did the survey find out about women?

a They like to shop in large department stores.   1 ....

b They always make a shopping list.   2 ....

c They tend to buy inexpensive shoes.   3 ....

d They save money by buying special offers.

e They like expensive boutiques.

3 The instructions tell you to write no more than THREE words. Think about why the answers to each question are incorrect. Match the reasons a–d.

a too many words   c not enough answers

b too many answers   d misunderstood the question word

Question	Answer
1 Where do young people in the city like to meet their friends?	at the shopping mall
2 What three things do most teenagers like to spend their money on?	music, clothes, cinema, computers
3 When do you go shopping?	to the supermarket
4 Name two places where you can buy food.	market stall

Practice for the test

Section 4

 Questions 1–4

You will hear the introduction to a lecture about consumer habits. Complete the notes with NO MORE THAN THREE WORDS AND/OR NUMBERS.

Spending money

Point 1

– three age groups:

- young people,
- families,
- (1) ....

Point 2

– male and female (2) ....

Three age groups are:

- young people aged (3) ....
- families aged from 30–55
- mature adults (4) ....

 Questions 5–7

Now you will hear the next part of the recording. Answer the question. Select THREE correct options from the list, a-g.

What do families spend their money on?

a furniture and household goods

b clothes, music and entertainment

c cars and outings

d electronic equipment

e gardening tools

f food, toys and outings

g cars and travelling

5 ....

6 ....

7 ....

 Questions 8–10

Now you will hear the last part of the recording. Answer the questions. Write NO MORE THAN THREE WORDS OR A NUMBER for eating in restaurants.

8 What do men spend twice as much as women on?

....

9 What do women spend most on? ....

10 Which group spends most on eating in restaurants? ....

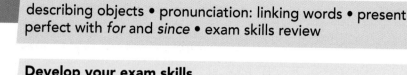

Speaking

describing objects • pronunciation: linking words • present perfect with *for* and *since* • exam skills review

Get READY for class!

Remember to do your preparation before class.

online • workbook

Develop your exam skills

1 **Read the tips below. Then complete the tips with the words in the box.**

> natural   notes   organize   pause

1 Try not to .... when you are answering – speak at a .... pace.

2 Make .... on each point on the task card.

3 Include useful phrases to .... your answer.

2 **Read the Part 2 task card below. Plan your answer for one minute using the tips from Exercise 1 to help you. Then record your answer.**

> **Describe a gift you bought for someone.**
>
> You should say:
>
> what it was
> who you bought it for
> why you bought it
>
> and say how you felt when you gave the gift.

3 **Read the tips below. Then complete them using the words in the box.**

> carefully   choose   tenses

1 Revise different grammatical .... and phrases from earlier units.

2 Listen .... to the examiner's questions and .... suitable tenses for your answer.

4 **Read the Part 3 questions below. Think about your answers using the tips from Exercise 3 to help you. Then record your answers.**

1 Do you think going shopping with friends is a good way to relax?

2 In your opinion, are there more advantages than disadvantages to studying in another country?

3 How has looking for a job changed compared to the past?

4 How should we encourage people to be active in their free time?

5 Read the tips below. Then complete them using the words in the box.

> adverbs   describing   repeat   similar   topic

1 Revise .... vocabulary from earlier units.
2 Do not .... words when you are .... something.
3 Try to use words with .... meanings, e.g. adjectives or ....

6 Read the Part 2 task card below. Plan your answer for one minute using the tips from Exercise 5 to help you. Then record your answer.

> **Talk about a photograph you took.**
>
> You should say:
>
> when you took it
> who was there
> what it shows
>
> and why you like this particular photograph.

Practice for the test

Part 1

 1 Listen to five Part 1 questions. Record your answer to each question.

Part 2

 2 Listen to and read the Part 2 task card below. Plan your answer. You have one minute for this in the exam. Then record your answer. You have one to two minutes for this in the exam.

> **Describe something you own which is very important to you.**
>
> You should say:
>
> what it is and what it looks like
> what it is made of
> how long you have had it
>
> and explain why it is important to you.

3 Answer the questions below to complete Part 2. Record your answer.

1 Would it be easy to replace this object?
2 Do your friends like this object?

Part 3

 4 Listen to four Part 3 questions. Answer the questions and record your answer.

Develop your exam skills

For a Task 2 essay you will often be asked to give your own opinion. You should also include a range of other opinions to show you understand both sides of an argument.

To give your own opinion, use phrases such as *In my view / opinion* and verb phrases such as *I think that / I believe that* … .

To show other people's opinions, use *According to* + group of people (e.g. *parents / scientists / politicians*) … .

Use verb phrases such as *Some people think that / Many people believe that / People argue that / Other people claim that* … . You can also use *suggest / state / say*.

1 **Read the sentences below. Decide if the opinions are the writer's or those of other people. Write WO (writer's opinion) or OPO (other people's opinion). Then underline the phrases that introduce each opinion.**

1 According to the government, traditional families are the happiest.

2 There are many things that can make people happy. In my view, family and friends are the most important.

3 Some teachers believe that children should learn how to manage money at school. They suggest that this could help the economy in the future.

4 I believe that the government should provide more financial help to poor families.

5 My personal opinion is that having an enjoyable job is essential for happiness.

6 Many people argue that all citizens should pay as little tax as possible.

7 I think that wealthy people should pay more tax.

8 Parents often claim that they need more money.

Exam tip

For Task 2 you should say briefly what your own opinion is in the introduction to your essay so that this is clear from the start.

see **GRAMMAR** page 159 and more **PRACTICE** online

2 **Read the essay title below and the introduction to the essay. Underline the phrases used to introduce the writer's opinion and the opinions of other people. Then answer the questions about the introduction that follow.**

If people have more money, they are generally happier. To what extent do you agree with this statement?

Money is important in life but it does not always bring happiness. Some people say that having more money makes life less stressful, while other people argue that happiness can be found in other aspects of life, such as work, family or hobbies. In my view, having more money does not make people happier but it makes life easier. There are two reasons for my opinion.

1 What do some people say? ....

2 What do other people argue? ....

3 What does the writer think? ....

4 How many reasons will the writer give for his / her opinion? ....

3 Read the following essay title and the notes below. Think about how you can use the notes to write an introduction. Then write an introduction using your own ideas. Remember to introduce the opinions of other people as well as your own ideas.

Personal happiness comes from being successful in life. How far do you agree with this statement?

happiness comes from:	religion
positive attitude to life	having lots of friends
being famous	life experiences – holidays, sports, hobbies
success in job	possessions – house, car, clothes

4 Read the paragraph below for the essay in Exercise 2. Think about whether each sentence or clause agrees or contrasts with what has just been said. Then complete the paragraph using suitable linking words.

Firstly, I believe that money makes life easier because it reduces stress and worry. Families who have enough money to spend on accommodation, food and clothing are less stressed and so have fewer arguments. (**1**) ...., children from wealthy families often do better at school (**2**) .... this may be because they can afford to pay for good schools. (**3**) ...., some people think that money cannot solve all family problems. (**4**) .... they believe that love from parents is more important than money for bringing up children. (**5**) ...., I think that it can be difficult for parents to be positive and loving if they are always worrying about money.

5 Read the beginning of the second paragraph and the notes in the box. Use the notes to think how to write the paragraph and add notes of your own. Then continue the paragraph giving your own opinions and the opinions of other people. Remember to use linking words correctly.

Secondly, having more money can help people plan for the future so they have more control over their lives. …

Saving money for children's education – children have better future
Getting a better job increases income – can buy more possessions – better life
Saving money for old age – less need to ask others for financial help

Your ideas:

6 **Read the following essay title and paragraph. Complete the paragraph with suitable referencing words, e.g. pronouns, this and that and linking words.**

Happiness is considered very important in life. What are the best ways to be happy?

One of the best ways to be happy is to try to develop a positive attitude to life. In my opinion, (1) .... approach can help people to reduce stress and negative feelings. (2) .... can be much happier simply by thinking about all the good things in their life: family, friends, good health and pets. They can (3) .... focus on improving things they are less happy about, such as getting a better job or moving to a new place. (4) ...., many other people say that (5) .... isn't easy for people who have serious money problems or no chance of changing their life. (6) .... factors can often cause people to have problems with stress and ill health. (7) .... problems can affect how happy someone is (8) .... staying positive can still help in these situations.

7 **Write one more paragraph for the essay in Exercise 6.**

Practice for the test

Task 2

You should spend about 40 minutes on this task.

Write about the following topic:

Friends and family bring more happiness than money and possessions. How far do you agree with this statement?

Give reasons for your answer and include any relevant examples from your own knowledge or experience.

Write at least 250 words.

Reading

Exam tip

Read the questions first, and then skim-read the text to get an idea of its structure, and scan for the specific information. Every paragraph usually has a sentence that summarizes the main idea(s) in the paragraph (the topic sentence). This sentence may help you.

Develop your exam skills

info In the exam, you may be asked to match specific information, for example, a reason, a description or an explanation, to the section of a text where you can find it, A, B, C, etc.

1 Read the text in Exercise 2. Match the underlined parts of the text to the type of specific information described in the box. Find two more reasons and one more explanation in the text.

> **1** explanation   **2** reason   **3** example   **4** comparison   **5** condition

2 Re-read paragraphs A, D and E. Then choose the best descriptions of the paragraphs, a, b or c. Decide which is the topic sentence for each paragraph.

1 *paragraph A*

   a the media   **b** large companies   **c** smaller businesses

2 *paragraph D*

   a the reasons why small companies are better than larger ones

   b the reasons why the government wants more small businesses

   c a list of good points about small companies

3 *paragraph E*

   a the role of policy makers

   b the importance of business planning

   c tips on improving your business

3 Read the questions below. Underline any key words in the questions. Then use the keywords to help you find answers in the text.

1 Which paragraph mentions statistics?

2 In paragraph A, which word indicates that the text will not be about large businesses?

3 In paragraph C, which sentence explains why new and developing small businesses are crucial to the success of the economy?

4 Which paragraph builds on the same idea as the one in A and C (mentioned in question 5)?

A The business sections of the media tend to focus on large, traditional companies. By definition, these are high-profile businesses – the companies that are quoted in the leading share price indices. However, most economists agree that smaller businesses, particularly new and developing small businesses, are central to the long-term success of any economy. They argue that the industries of the future will originate in the small business sector. That is why the United Nations Economic Commission for Europe describes SMEs (small and medium-sized enterprises, with fewer than 250 employees) as 'the engine of economic development'.

B In the UK, the Department of Trade and Industry (DTI) reported that the total number of businesses, including small companies, partnerships and sole traders, rose by 260,000 in 2004 to 4.3 million (source: www.dti.gov.uk). This is up from the previous year and represents the best figures ever recorded.

C This is success for government policy. Successive UK governments have sought to encourage small business start-ups. Behind the policy is a belief that small businesses contribute to a stronger economic base, and that they have the ability to thrive in a competitive global business environment.

D The government also encourages small businesses because they are:

- a source of employment
- flexible and innovative
- responsive to gaps in the market
- able to accommodate people with a passion for a product and who might not thrive in a large corporation.

Business planning

E Policy makers recognize that it is not sufficient to simply encourage an enterprise culture. If new entrepreneurs are to succeed, if new businesses are to thrive, then it is important that they appreciate the central role of planning. A business plan is the basis of new business development, and it encourages an entrepreneur to think ahead and plan, as far as possible, for the business to be successful.

F Writing a business plan will not in itself ensure that a business survives. However, it is an invaluable exercise, forcing entrepreneurs to go through planning steps to make sure their business propositions are viable. A business plan draws on concepts, skills and knowledge, including:

- doing market research to make sure that planned products and services meet customer needs
- understanding the market by analysing competitors' products, services and prices
- setting clear business aims and objectives
- finding sufficient capital to meet the business's short-term and long-term needs
- deciding on the most suitable structure and form of ownership for the business.

Glossary

share price indices: plural of 'share price index': a system by which (the speed of) changes in the value of share prices is recorded and measured • *sole trader:* a person who owns their own business and does not have a partner or any shareholders

---

Practice for the test

Questions 1–6

The passage below has nine paragraphs A–I. Which paragraphs mention the following information? You may use any letter more than once.

1 physical and mental problems that a business owner can face ....

2 leadership and team improvement ideas ....

3 the advantage of not expanding in business ....

4 individuals and larger groups that can help people new to business ....

5 the reasons why the more basic jobs in a small company should not be carried out by employers ....

6 external reasons why companies should try to keep their employees' knowledge and expertise up-to-date ....

Setting up in business

A It takes a considerable commitment to set up and run a small business. Owners must be able to do all the tasks necessary to run the business or have sufficient funds to buy in appropriate external help; and even then they must be able to check the quality of the service they are receiving.

B Anyone planning to start a business must be realistic about what can be achieved, and in what time frame. Entrepreneurs often work extremely long hours, not just during 'trading' hours, but also after hours doing all the associated paperwork. If entrepreneurs overwork, they will find it difficult to make good decisions and will lack the energy to analyse and evaluate marketing and finance data. If an entrepreneur becomes over-tired and over-anxious, they can undermine their businesses by giving the impression that things are bad and the business is just about to close down.

C Many organizations provide support networks for entrepreneurs running small businesses. These networks provide training and access to experienced business mentors for little or no charge. The Business Link network, funded by Department of Trade and Industry, is one source of this kind of support. If entrepreneurs are under 30 years of age, the Prince's Trust also provides training and mentoring for business start-ups. There are various other privately run business networking groups which can be both fun and mutually supportive.

D Owners need to consider four key issues: training, leadership and team development, delegation and management systems.

E Investment in training is necessary to ensure that staff have the skills to do their jobs efficiently and they can meet the requirements of current legislation, such as health and safety. Staff may also need training to develop skills to meet internationally recognized quality standards for products and service delivery. Research shows that small and medium-sized firms often find it very difficult to organize effective training.

F Ideally, workplace teams should be happy, creative working groups of individuals who support each other, work to each other's strengths and work towards the business's goals. This might require the owners to undertake self-assessment and target-setting reviews to ensure that the business is staying focused on its objectives. Team development can be fostered by organizing events such as team lunches and days out walking together.

G Owners should delegate and employ appropriate people to do the tasks that they cannot do or do not have time to do. By freeing themselves from some of the easier day-to-day tasks of the business, owners can spend their time monitoring the overall business and thinking about where the business should be going. Certainly, if the owners are passionate about the business, they need time to step back and focus on the long-term goals and vision of the organization. They also need time to network, to build up sales leads and to explore further investment opportunities for the business.

H In time, owners need to be able to let go of control of some aspects of the business and to develop more formal management systems. This is probably the most difficult task for any entrepreneur. Many entrepreneurs find it very difficult to trust paid employees to run their businesses.

I At this stage in their development, without outside help and guidance, many businesses simply reach their 'natural' capacity and they do not develop or grow any further. Entrepreneurs need to decide whether they want to keep their business small – so that they retain control of all decisions – or whether they want to go on growing their business and therefore accept that this will necessarily change their role in the business.

Glossary

Business Link: the UK government's online resource to provide support for businesses • *Prince's Trust:* a charity in the UK started by Prince Charles in 1976 to help young people

Practice test

In this section, you will find an example of an IELTS exam. You will also find the official answer sheets for the Listening and Reading tests on pages 139 and 140. Taking this practice test under timed conditions will give you an idea of what it will be like to take the actual exam.

You have 30 minutes to complete the Listening test and you have an extra 10 minutes to transfer your answers to the answer sheet. There are four sections.

SECTION 1

Questions 1–3

 Answer the questions below. Choose the correct letter, a, b or c.

Example: How long does the caller want to go away for?

  a a week   **b** a few weeks   **ⓒ** a few days

1 Where does the caller want to stay?

  a in the country   **b** in the city   **c** by the beach

2 What kind of hotel does the caller want to stay in?

  a a family hotel   **b** a spa   **c** a farmhouse

3 Which hotel does the caller choose?

  a Sparkling Springs   **b** Farmhouse Getaways   **c** Ocean Waves Resort

 ### Questions 4–7

Complete the form below. Write NO MORE THAN THREE WORDS AND/OR A NUMBER for each answer.

Hotel Reservation Form	
Name:	William French
Billing Address:	**(2)** ....
	Standmarch
	Norfolk
	NE1 4SP
Mobile Number:	**(5)** ....
Check-in Date:	15th June
Check-out Date:	**(6)** ....
Payment Type:	Credit card
Amount:	**(7)** £ ....

Questions 8–10

Complete the map below. Write NO MORE THAN THREE WORDS AND/OR A NUMBER for each answer.

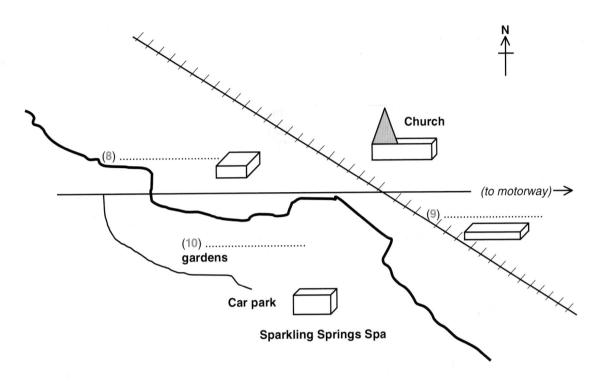

SECTION 2

Questions 11–13

Answer the questions below. Write NO MORE THAN THREE WORDS AND/OR A NUMBER for each answer.

11 Which exhibition does the tour guide recommend?

12 How long do the guided tours last?

13 On which floor do the tours start?

Questions 14–17

Match the sections of the museum with the age group they are recommended for. Write A–C next to 14–17.

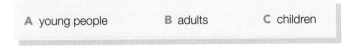

A young people   **B** adults   **C** children

14 shapes and patterns

15 the history of flight

16 energy

17 exploring physics

Questions 18–20

Complete the flow chart below. Write **NO MORE THAN THREE WORDS AND/OR A NUMBER** for each answer.

How to buy a ticket for an exhibition:

Choose the 'events' button on the museum home page

↓

Click on the
(18) ....

↓

Choose the date on the
(19) ....

↓

Choose the time and the
(20) ....

↓

Select payment method.

SECTION 3

 Questions 21–23

Complete the notes below. Write **NO MORE THAN THREE WORDS AND/OR A NUMBER** for each answer.

Focus of survey: **(21)** .... preferences
Number of questions: 20
Information required in first three questions: cost, number of rooms and **(22)** ....
Topic of additional information: **(23)** ....

 Questions 24–26

Choose THREE letters, a–g.

Which THREE ways does the tutor suggest Monica and Tom can improve their questionnaire?

a   make the questions shorter

b   make the questions simpler

c   increase the number of questions   24 ....

d   ask more questions about the students' homes   25 ....

e   not to ask so many questions   26 ....

f   ask for more explanations

g   ask more questions about cost

Questions 27–30

Complete the diagram below. Write **NO MORE THAN THREE WORDS AND/OR A NUMBER** for each answer.

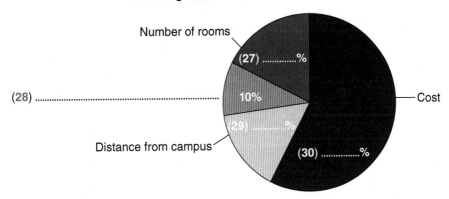

Choosing Accommodation

Number of rooms

(27) ....%

(28) ....

10%

Cost

(29) ....%

Distance from campus

(30) ....%

SECTION 4

Questions 31–34

Complete the summary of the introduction to a lecture on bird migration below. Write **NO MORE THAN THREE WORDS AND/OR A NUMBER** for each answer.

Birds migrate for two main reasons: to (**31**) .... and to breed. When they are breeding, they need to move to areas where they can (**32**) .... In the spring they migrate from (**33**) .... to cooler countries in the north. They spend several months there, flying south again in the winter to (**34**) ....

Questions 35–37

Answer the questions below. Write NO MORE THAN THREE WORDS AND/OR A NUMBER for each answer.

35 How has global warming affected the arrival of spring?

36 Why have birds started to migrate earlier?

37 What happens to the population of birds that breed late?

Questions 38–40

Choose THREE letters, A–F.

Match each geographical area with a migration pattern.

A migration to warm countries	**D** partial migration
B clockwise migration	**E** migration to countries with long days
C long distance migration	**F** circular migration around entire globe

38 the tropics ....

39 the Arctic and Antarctic ....

40 North America ....

Speaking

The Speaking test is in three parts and you have 11–14 minutes to complete it.

Listen to the examiner and answer the questions in each part.

 PART 1

1 Do you work or are you a student?
2 Do you have a large family?
3 Describe your hometown.
4 What's the weather like in your country?
5 What are some of your hobbies?

 PART 2

> **Describe a person who helped you.**
>
> You should say:
>
> where you met the person
> what relationship you had with this person
> what was special about them
>
> and explain how this person helped you.

Would you like to help someone in this way?

 PART 3

1 Do you think we can learn anything from older generations?
2 Compare the role of the family in today's world to the past.
3 Should we ask our family for help, or should we try to be independent?
4 In your opinion, when does a child become an adult?

You have one hour to complete the Reading test. This includes the time required to write your answers on an answer sheet. There are three passages, so aim to spend about twenty minutes on each of them.

READING PASSAGE 1

You should spend about 20 minutes on questions 1–14, which are based on Reading passage 1 below.

Is this the end of the High Street?

Take a walk down any 'High Street', normally places full of shops, and you'll notice signs that all is not well: they will say 'To Let'.

The High Street faces real competition from out-of-town retail parks and the steady growth of supermarkets, both in number and in size. There is also the growing trend for people to shop online, combined with a reduction in many families' finances, which has affected customer confidence.

Retailing (the sale of goods from a fixed location) is changing too: shopping is becoming a leisure activity as much as a necessity, along with the rise of home delivery services saving time and journeys. Convenience is a powerful motivator for shoppers' behaviour. Is the traditional High Street dying out?

During the last two years, independent retailers have struggled more than the chain stores. Research suggests over 12,000 independent stores closed in 2009. Economies of scale (it is cheaper to buy stock in bulk, so big shops can charge lower prices) are one part of the issue.

Supermarkets have a stronger control over the supply chain and can manipulate prices more effectively. As a result of the decline in smaller stores, there are now many empty shops in most town centres, some of which have been vacant for some time, and have whitewashed windows. What impact do they have on the overall 'feel' of the town for visitors and residents?

More importantly, how does the loss of a familiar shop, which has perhaps served decades of local residents, affect people at a time when so many other familiar aspects of daily life are under threat? When a shopping mall is being planned, it is very important to secure the key 'anchor' tenants: the big names that can guarantee customers through the doors. Is the disappearance of these familiar local shops and small department stores like losing a link with the past?

The growth of CCTV cameras, use of private security firms and blurring of public and private land has also been an issue in cities such as Exeter. This can result in young people feeling that they are being victimized and forced out of city centres.

Another feature of many city centres is that they are beginning to look very similar to each other. The New Economics Foundation introduced the term 'clone town' in a report published in 2004. This suggests that many High Streets have few individual characteristics – the same shops can be seen in most towns. This was also followed up by a report in 2010, which identified Cambridge as the most 'cloned' city in the UK: one with very few independent stores in the centre.

Vacant shops are another issue for town centres. These can end up as charity shops, 'pop-up' shops (especially around Christmas) or attract vandals and graffiti. Some cities such as Portsmouth have made an effort to revamp empty store-fronts to improve those areas where they are found. This is important for cities which attract large numbers of tourists, such as Bath, York and Chester.

Services are perhaps more resilient to these changes, particularly those that offer something that is not available online. As one person commented: 'You can't have your hair cut online …' – well, not yet anyway. This partly explains the growth of coffee shops and nail bars in some town centres, which are going against the general trend.

Finally, out on the edges of our towns, the supermarkets continue to grow – they've got the town centre surrounded. A report published in late 2010 said that around 55p of every £1 that we spend is spent in supermarkets, and there have been a large number of planning applications for further stores.

Glossary

The High Street: (British) the main street of a town, usually where the principal shops are situated

QUESTIONS 1–6

Do the following statements agree with the views of the writer? Write:

YES if the statement agrees with the views of the writer

NO if the statement contradicts what the writer thinks

NOT GIVEN if it is impossible to know what the writer's point of view is

1 Not only are supermarkets getting bigger, there are more of them than ever. ....

2 People have less money now, so they try to buy cheaper goods via the Internet. ....

3 People shop because they have to, but also because it is fun. ....

4 The younger generation may feel unwelcome in certain towns. ....

5 Although most towns have the same shops, there are many features that make them unique.

....

6 Although a large number of stores are closing, the number of shops that offer services is increasing.

....

QUESTIONS 7–10

Look at the following features, 7–10, and the list of groups below. Match each item with the correct group, A–D.

NB You may use any letter more than once.

7 there are fewer of them ....

8 competition is increasing ....

9 business is getting better ....

10 they are often located outside the city centre ....

This is true for:

> A independent shops that sell goods
>
> B supermarkets
>
> C both supermarkets and independent shops
>
> D private security firms

QUESTIONS 11–14

Choose the appropriate letters, a–d, to finish sentences 11–14.

11 Britain's High Streets are

    a full of shops.

    b suffering because of online shopping.

    c convenient for shoppers.

    d providing more competition for chain stores.

12 Economies of scale

    a are causing problems for independent shops.

    b means that bigger shops can buy more goods.

    c affected 12,000 independent stores in 2009.

    d are responsible for the economic problems of the past two years.

13 Shopping malls

    a are being built in High Streets.

    b are increasingly using CCTV.

    c are being planned in Cambridge.

    d like having well-known shops.

14 Nail bars

    a are no longer trendy.

    b are becoming more popular.

    c are starting to offer online services.

    d are also starting to cut hair.

11 ....   12 ....   13 ....   14 ....

READING PASSAGE 2

You should spend about 20 minutes on questions 15–27, which are based on Reading passage 2 below.

London's cycle hire scheme

A London is a 'world city': one of the most important economic and financial hubs in the world. It has a population of around eight million people and contains hundreds of iconic buildings which are recognized the world over. London receives around 20 million visitors each year, a large proportion from overseas, who mingle with further millions of people who travel into the city from a wide area to work in the central area. It is frequently rated as providing the most satisfying 'cultural experience' for visitors to any city.

B One of the challenges involved in managing (and living in) such a huge city is the ability to move people efficiently around it for the purposes of work and leisure, and at reasonable cost. The London black cab is one response to this problem, but it also contributes to the number of vehicles that are on the roads. The much quoted result of millions of daily vehicle movements is a very low average speed for traffic on London's roads and frequent congestion problems.

C Many cities have taken steps to reduce the amount of traffic on the roads by adopting a range of measures which can broadly be described as either 'carrots' or 'sticks': those which either promote, or discourage certain activity. London has already been forced into trying a number of measures to reduce traffic congestion. These have included:

- traffic management systems which included the world's first traffic light. It was installed outside the Houses of Parliament in 1868 to reduce congestion in this area.

- an underground system which was the first in the world. The first section opened in 1863, and the network is still developing. Since 2003, it has been managed by Transport for London. The classic London Tube map forms part of the city's cultural heritage, and has been much copied and adapted elsewhere.

- the Cross Rail development, due to provide high frequency rail services through two new tunnels under Central London from 2017.

- the congestion charging system; introduced in 2003 and extended in 2007, it charges many motorists (there are some exemptions) £10 to enter the central charging zone between 7 a.m. and 6 p.m., Monday to Friday.

- the Oyster card: an automated charging system which speeds up the use of public transport; this is a specially chipped card, which can be pre-charged with 'credit'.

D The latest solution is the Santander London Cycle Hire Scheme. In 2010, London joined a growing list of cities that had turned to the bicycle for a possible solution to traffic congestion. Cities like Amsterdam have long been associated with bicycles. Other cities that already have cycle hire schemes include Copenhagen and Barcelona.

In Paris, the system is known as the Velib scheme, a word which merges the French words for *bicycle* and *freedom*. It is funded by advertising. The London scheme was launched on 30th July 2010 with an initial total of 5,000 bikes spread around 315 locations, and with plans for further extensions. The bikes are fairly robust so that they can withstand the knocks of daily use. They are fitted with dynamo-powered LED lights, have three gears, a chain guard and a bell. Each bike is also fitted with a Radio Frequency Identification (RFID) chip, so that its location can be tracked. The bikes have puncture-proof tyres and are regularly checked over for mechanical faults.

E It is hoped that people will experience London in a more direct way. Instead of descending into the earth, they will cycle the streets and thus gain 'a different view' of London and improve their own mental maps of the city. They will also be getting exercise, which in an age of soaring obesity rates can only be a good thing, can't it?

F Enough reading, time for you to get out there and start pedalling!

Glossary

the Tube: the underground railway system in London

QUESTIONS 15–18

Choose one of the endings, i–viii, from the list of endings to complete each sentence below. The information in the completed sentences should accurately reflect what is said in the text.

NB There are more endings (i–viii) than sentence beginnings, so you will not need to use them all. You may use each ending once only.

15 London ....

16 London traffic ....

17 The London Cycle hire scheme ....

18 The London Underground ....

List of endings

  i has influenced others.

 ii has twenty millions foreign visitors a year.

 iii is not an original idea.

 iv is a place where travellers can feel safe.

  v is not organized as well as it is elsewhere.

 vi is slow.

 vii has had to try to solve traffic problems.

viii causes pollution.

QUESTIONS 19–23

Reading passage 2 has five sections, A–E.

Choose the most suitable headings for sections A–E from the list of headings below. Write the appropriate numbers, i–ix, next to the sections.

NB There are more headings than sections, so you will not use them all.

19   Section A ....
20   Section B ....
21   Section C ....
22   Section D ....
23   Section E ....

> **List of headings**
>
> i   Current and past actions
>
> ii   Congestion and pollution
>
> iii   Problems on the roads
>
> iv   The best city in the world
>
> v   A centre of activity
>
> vi   The many benefits of cycling
>
> vii   Cycling in European cities
>
> viii   A new initiative
>
> ix   Rail systems

QUESTIONS 24–27

Complete the summary below, each time with **ONE WORD** from Reading passage 2.

The Santander Cycles Hire Scheme was started in 2010 in the hope of providing a
(24) .... for the existing transport issues. The money that was necessary to have a scheme like this was sourced from
(25) .... and allowed London to have 5,000 bikes initially, but there are likely to be
(26) .... to the scheme. The bikes have a tracking
(27) ...., are properly equipped and regularly maintained.

READING PASSAGE 3

You should spend about 20 minutes on questions 28–40, which are based on Reading passage 3 below.

Personalized exercise

At the start of every new year, many of us promise ourselves that a certain number of times a week we will go to the gym, go jogging, attend an exercise class, etc. But many of us struggle to fit exercise into our lives, or we start off well and then give up.

The key could be to find the right type of exercise for you. After all, if we end up doing something we enjoy and can see the benefits of, we are more likely to carry on for longer than a few weeks. Studies suggest that six weeks are all it takes to form a habit, so once we have managed to continue for that length of time, chances are that exercise has become a routine part of our lives that we do not question. So what exercise is right for you? Read on to find out.

First of all, you need to determine your motivation. Are you mainly interested in de-stressing or in getting fitter? If your ultimate goal is relaxation, then ask yourself if you want to do this energetically, in which case a type of martial art or exercise based on boxing may be right for you. If you have a calmer style, then you could choose solitary exercise, such as walking the dog, doing some gardening, or opting for a brisk daily walk around the block. If you get more motivated from working with others, then you could join a yoga, pilates or t'ai chi class, all designed to stretch and strengthen your muscles and with the added benefit of calming the mind.

If it is fitness and weight loss you are after, then group activities include military fitness, typically organized in local parks, walking and running groups, dance classes (try line dancing, tap dancing or ballet). Contact your local council for details of those. On your own, you could go horse riding, swimming, or if you fear that you will choose not to leave your house, download fitness and motivational exercise programmes that you can do at home.

Finally, even people who are incredibly busy have no excuse. It is getting easier to fit exercise into our lives, rather than having to make so many changes to our lifestyles that we are doomed to fail. If you have particular time slots available, then you could book some time at the weekend with a personal trainer who can come to your house, or you could meet them at the gym. During the week, you could use the daily commute for your exercise, by walking faster, parking the car further away from work, or getting your bicycle out. If your life is not as regular, you could choose the next couple of minutes you have spare to try an exercise DVD, or get the skipping ropes out and do some skipping. You could also go outdoors to your nearest fitness trail, or put your running shoes on and run for any length of time, as everything counts when you are doing exercise.

You see? There is no excuse. Whatever your lifestyle, you will be able to find something that suits you. Just sit down with a cup of tea, read this article again, have a think about your options. Then finish the tea, get up, get going, and don't stop.

QUESTIONS 28–33

Use **NO MORE THAN THREE WORDS** from the passage to complete each blank in the diagram below.

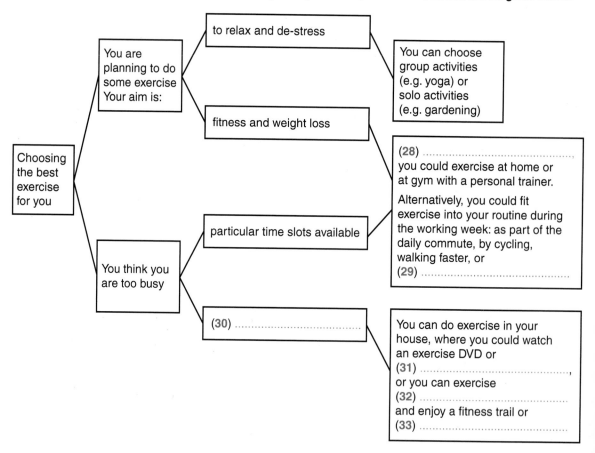

QUESTIONS 34–36

Reading passage 3 has six paragraphs, A–F. Which paragraphs state the following information? Write the appropriate letters A–F next to numbers 34–36.

NB There are more paragraphs than summaries, so you will not use them all.

34 It is recommendable to take action without delay.

35 Suitable exercise is more long term.

36 Get fitter wherever you are.

QUESTIONS 37–38

Using NO MORE THAN THREE WORDS from the text for each, answer the following questions.

37 What kind of activity do people who would rather exercise alone prefer?

38 Who can provide information about organized sports or fitness activities with others?

QUESTIONS 39–40

Do the following statements agree with the information in the passage? Write:

TRUE if the text confirms the statement

FALSE if the text contradicts the statement

NOT GIVEN if it is impossible to know from the text

39 It is important to try to exercise for six weeks without giving up.

40 Having a cup of tea is part of a healthy lifestyle.

You have one hour to complete the Writing test. This section has two parts and you should spend about 20 minutes on Task 1 and 40 minutes on Task 2.

WRITING TASK 1

You should spend about 20 minutes on this task.

The bar chart below shows the types of music bought in the USA in 2010, by age group. Summarize the information by selecting and reporting the main features, and make comparisons where relevant.

Write at least 150 words.

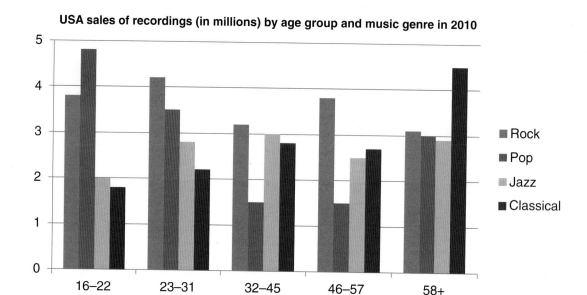

USA sales of recordings (in millions) by age group and music genre in 2010

WRITING TASK 2

You should spend about 40 minutes on this task.

Write about the following topic:

Students are becoming more and more reliant on the Internet. While the Internet is convenient, it has many negative effects and its use for educational purposes should be restricted.

How far do you agree with this statement?

Give reasons for your answer and include any relevant examples from your own knowledge or experience.

Write at least 250 words.

IELTS Listening and Reading Answer Sheet

Centre number:

Pencil must be used to complete this sheet.

Please write your **full name** in CAPITAL letters on the line below:

_____

Then write your six digit Candidate number in the boxes and shade the number in the grid on the right.

0 1 2 3 4 5 6 7 8 9
0 1 2 3 4 5 6 7 8 9
0 1 2 3 4 5 6 7 8 9
0 1 2 3 4 5 6 7 8 9
0 1 2 3 4 5 6 7 8 9
0 1 2 3 4 5 6 7 8 9

Test date (shade ONE box for the day, ONE box for the month and ONE box for the year):

Day: 01 02 03 04 05 06 07 08 09 10 11 12 13 14 15 16 17 18 19 20 21 22 23 24 25 26 27 28 29 30 31

Month: 01 02 03 04 05 06 07 08 09 10 11 12   Year (last 2 digits): 13 14 15 16 17 18 19 20 21

| Listening | Listening | Listening | Listening | Listening | Listening |

#	Answer	Marker use only	#	Answer	Marker use only
1		✓ 1 ✗	21		✓ 21 ✗
2		✓ 2 ✗	22		✓ 22 ✗
3		✓ 3 ✗	23		✓ 23 ✗
4		✓ 4 ✗	24		✓ 24 ✗
5		✓ 5 ✗	25		✓ 25 ✗
6		✓ 6 ✗	26		✓ 26 ✗
7		✓ 7 ✗	27		✓ 27 ✗
8		✓ 8 ✗	28		✓ 28 ✗
9		✓ 9 ✗	29		✓ 29 ✗
10		✓ 10 ✗	30		✓ 30 ✗
11		✓ 11 ✗	31		✓ 31 ✗
12		✓ 12 ✗	32		✓ 32 ✗
13		✓ 13 ✗	33		✓ 33 ✗
14		✓ 14 ✗	34		✓ 34 ✗
15		✓ 15 ✗	35		✓ 35 ✗
16		✓ 16 ✗	36		✓ 36 ✗
17		✓ 17 ✗	37		✓ 37 ✗
18		✓ 18 ✗	38		✓ 38 ✗
19		✓ 19 ✗	39		✓ 39 ✗
20		✓ 20 ✗	40		✓ 40 ✗

| Marker 2 Signature | | Marker 1 Signature | | Listening Total |

IELTS L-R v1.0

denote Print Limited 0121 520 5100

DP787/394

Reproduced with permission of Cambridge English Language Assessment ©UCLES 2016

Please write your **full name** in CAPITAL letters on the line below:

_____

Please write your Candidate number on the line below:

_____

Please write your three digit language code in the boxes and shade the numbers in the grid on the right.

0 1 2 3 4 5 6 7 8 9
0 1 2 3 4 5 6 7 8 9
0 1 2 3 4 5 6 7 8 9

Are you: Female? ⏤   Male? ⏤

Reading   Reading   Reading   Reading   Reading   Reading

Module taken (shade one box):   Academic ⏤   General Training ⏤

	Marker use only			Marker use only
1	✓ 1 ✗	21		✓ 21 ✗
2	✓ 2 ✗	22		✓ 22 ✗
3	✓ 3 ✗	23		✓ 23 ✗
4	✓ 4 ✗	24		✓ 24 ✗
5	✓ 5 ✗	25		✓ 25 ✗
6	✓ 6 ✗	26		✓ 26 ✗
7	✓ 7 ✗	27		✓ 27 ✗
8	✓ 8 ✗	28		✓ 28 ✗
9	✓ 9 ✗	29		✓ 29 ✗
10	✓ 10 ✗	30		✓ 30 ✗
11	✓ 11 ✗	31		✓ 31 ✗
12	✓ 12 ✗	32		✓ 32 ✗
13	✓ 13 ✗	33		✓ 33 ✗
14	✓ 14 ✗	34		✓ 34 ✗
15	✓ 15 ✗	35		✓ 35 ✗
16	✓ 16 ✗	36		✓ 36 ✗
17	✓ 17 ✗	37		✓ 37 ✗
18	✓ 18 ✗	38		✓ 38 ✗
19	✓ 19 ✗	39		✓ 39 ✗
20	✓ 20 ✗	40		✓ 40 ✗

Marker 2 Signature	Marker 1 Signature	Reading Total

Grammar guide

Describing people and things

Posessive 's and s' (see page 7)
Using 's to show who things belong to

You use noun + **'s**:

- with a name.
  Stephanie is Michael's wife.
- with a singular noun (usually people).
  My brother wants to borrow Dad's car.
- with an irregular plural noun.
  People's lives are interesting.
  My uncles sell men's and women's clothes.
- for people's homes and common places.
  I go to my cousin Suzy's at the weekend.
  Kim works at the doctor's.

Words ending in 's

With words ending in s, you add **'s**.
  This is James's room.

Regular plural nouns

With regular plural nouns you add an apostrophe.
  My friends' house is on a mountain.

More than one noun

With more than one noun, you add **'s** after the second person.
  Jack and Jen's mother is my cousin.

Possessive pronouns

You use possessive pronouns (**mine, yours, his, hers, ours, theirs**) when you talk about who things belong to.
  *It's not my DVD. It's **his**.*
  *See that car over there. It's **ours**.*
  *Give me back that book. It's **mine**!*

You can also use **of** before a possessive pronoun.
  *I know Fiona very well. She's a very good friend **of mine**.*
  *Is it true that our new teacher is a neighbour **of yours**?*

Subject pronoun	Possessive pronoun
I	mine
you	yours
he	his
she	hers
we	ours
they	theirs

You use **one** and **ones** as pronouns for things.

  A: *I've got a few DVDs here. What do you want to watch?*
  B: *Well, this **one** is really funny. Let's watch that.*
  A: *These trainers all look the same. Which **ones** are yours?*
  B: *The **ones** with the green stripes.*

You can use **no** before a singular or a plural noun.
  *There were **no** people at the tennis courts yesterday.*
  *There was **no** food left at the end of the party.*

None (of) is always followed by a plural verb.
  ***None of** my friends are going to the concert next week.*
  *I need to go shopping. **None of** my clothes fit me.*

Adjectives (see pages 7, 37 and 68)

When you want to describe people or things, you can use the verb **be** and an adjective.
  I'm cold.
  She's kind.

You can use adverbs like **very** and **really** in front of many adjectives.
  *Paul's **very tall**.*
  *These questions are **really important**.*

You often need to use a preposition after some common adjectives.

Preposition	Adjective
at	good at, the worst at
of	fond of, afraid of

Preposition	Adjective
with	angry with, friendly with
about	worried about, excited about
to	kind to, unkind to

*I was always **good at** maths at school.*

*My mum's really **afraid of** spiders.*

*I was late for school and my teacher was **angry with** me.*

*I'm really **excited about** my holidays.*

*Sam was very **kind to** me on my first day at work.*

*My brother's **better** at tennis than me.*

Linking adjectives

When you use two adjectives of the same type, you use **and** to link them. With three or more adjectives, you link the last two with **and**, and put commas after the others.

*Anna is small **and** shy.*

*The boys are tall**,** dark **and** handsome.*

When you link two negative adjectives, you use **or**.

*My brother isn't mature **or** sensible.*

*We went to see a romantic comedy at the cinema. Unfortunately, it wasn't funny **or** romantic!*

Talking about free time and routines

Talking about what you like and don't like
(see page 19)

like, enjoy, love   not like, hate

> *Remember!*
>
> **Love** is stronger than **like** and **enjoy**.
>
> **Hate** is stronger than **not like**.

like, enjoy		
positive	**negative**	**+ -ing**
I **like/enjoy**	I **don't like/enjoy**	skiing.
He **likes/enjoys**	She **doesn't like/ enjoy**	cooking.

love, hate		
positive	**negative**	**+ -ing**
I **love**	I **hate**	shopping.
She **loves**	He **hates**	watching films.

Asking questions

Use the auxiliary verb **do/does**.

> ***Do** you **like** cooking?*
>
> ***Does** he **like** running?*
>
> ***Do** they **like** watching films?*
>
> *You don't usually ask questions with **love** or **hate**.*
>
> ~~*Do you love swimming? Do you hate studying?*~~

Prefer

You can use **prefer** when you want to say that you like one thing more than another thing.

> *Do you **prefer** watching TV **or** going to the cinema?*
>
> *I **prefer** walking **to** running.*

Verbs for talking about habits and ongoing situations **(see page 10)**

You use the **present simple**:

- for things that are always true.

  *My name **is** Jamil. I **come** from Morocco.*

  *I **have** two brothers.*

- for facts about your life.

  *I **work** in a shop.*

  *Beverly **lives** in an apartment.*

- to talk about habits and routines:

  *I **never go** swimming. I **often have** sandwiches for lunch. Steven **plays** tennis **every weekend**.*

> *Remember!*
>
> For **he**, **she** and **it**, add **-s** to the verb: *I **work**, you **work**, he/she/it **works**, we **work**, they **work**.*
>
> You use **does/doesn't** in negatives, questions and short answers.

Using adverbs to say how often you do something **(see page 53)**

We use frequency adverbs to clarify how often we do things.

0%   100%

never   sometimes   often   usually   always

You normally put the adverb before the verb in statements and questions.

> I **often** go to the cinema.
>
> I **never** listen to rock music.
>
> I s**ometimes** play computer games.
>
> Do you **often** play computer games?
>
> Does your sister **always** go out on Saturday nights?
>
> Do they **sometimes** go skiing?

But the adverb goes after the verb **be.**

> I'm **often** tired in the evenings.
>
> He was **never** late for class.
>
> Are you **ever** worried about the exam?

Here are some other frequency adverbs:

occasionally = sometimes but not often

> We **occasionally** go to restaurants but we usually eat at home.

normally = usually

I **normally** get home at six.

every day

I go to work **every day** except Sundays.

at weekends

Many people watch football **at weekends**.

all the time = very often

It's a great shop. I go there **all the time**.

Prepositions for when things happen

(see page 38)

in

in spring, summer, autumn, winter

in May, June, December

in 1974, **in** 2020

Come back **in** three months.

on

on Monday, Thursday, Sunday

on my birthday

on 30th April

at

at four o'clock

at 1.25 p.m.

before

I have breakfast **before** I go to school.
(1 breakfast, 2 school)

Mum walks the dog **before** she goes to work.
(1 walk dog, 2 work)

after

I do my homework **after** school. (1 school, 2 homework)

Vanessa goes dancing **after** dinner. (1 dinner, 2 dancing)

for

Wait here **for** a minute.

I practise the violin **for** five hours a week.

by

I need to be at the station **by** three o clock. (= I need to be at the station before or at three o'clock, not after three o'clock.)

Give me your homework **by** Friday. (= Give me your homework on Friday or before Friday, but not after Friday.)

during

During my holidays, I had fun with my friends. (= I had fun with my friends while I was on my holidays.)

The phone always rings **during** dinner! (= The phone always rings when we are having dinner.)

> ### Remember!
>
> You don't use **during** to say how long. You use **for**.
>
> > My parents are in France **for** three weeks.
> >
> > ~~My parents are in France **during** three weeks.~~

until/till

The post office is open from 9 a.m. **until/till** 4.30 p.m. (from 9 a.m. to 4.30 p.m.)

Let's wait **till** Maria gets here.

last/this/next

You use **last** for the past.

> **Last** year I went to Spain.

You use **this** for now.

> **This** week I am busy.

You use **next** for the future.

> **Next** week it's my birthday.

Times and dates

You write the time like this:

> 9 a.m., 10.10 a.m., 3.30 p.m., 7.45 p.m., 9.35 p.m.

You use **a.m.** for the morning and **p.m.** for the afternoon and evening.

> Midnight is 12.00 **a.m.** and midday is 12.00 **p.m.**

You say the time like this:

It's nine o'clock. It's ten past ten. It's half past three. / It's three thirty. It's quarter to eight / It's seven forty-five. It's twenty-five to ten. / It's nine thirty-five.

You can write the date in different ways:

Thursday 20th November

Friday, 13 September, 2016

29th April 1761

You use ordinal numbers with dates when you say the date:

*My birthday is on the **twelfth** of May.*

Questions and requests

Direct and indirect questions in the present and past (see pages 10, 17 and 22)

Direct questions

You can use question words to make wh questions: **when, where, which, what, who, how, why** and **whose.**

When *did you last go shopping?*

Where *did you go last weekend?*

Which *parts of the newspaper do you read?*

What *were you doing yesterday evening?*

Who *do you look like in your family?*

How *tall is he/she?*

Why *do you like him/her?*

Whose *books are those?*

Indirect questions

You can also ask indirect questions. These can sound more polite.

Do you know where the post office is? (= Where is the post office?)

Did you understand what he was saying? (= What was he saying?)

Can you tell me when the bank opens? (= When does the bank open?)

You use **which** when you are asking about a small number of things.

Which *dress do you prefer?*

Which *programme do you want to watch?*

You use **how** to ask for instructions to do something.

How *do you turn the computer on?*

*Can you tell me **how** I can get a passport?*

To find out who something belongs to, you use **whose.**

*A: **Whose** car is that outside?*

B: It's mine.

*Do you know **whose** those gloves are?*

To find out what someone thinks about a person or thing, you can use **what ... like.**

*A: **What's** their new CD **like**?*

B: It's great.

*A: **What's** your new teacher **like**?*

B: She's quite nice but she's a bit strict.

Remember!

Look carefully at the word order and different verb forms in direct and indirect questions.

*When **does** the supermarket **open**?*

***Do you know** when the supermarket **opens**?*

Making requests

To make requests, you can use these phrases:

- to ask someone to do something.

  *A: **Can** you explain that again, please? B: Yes, of course.*

  *A: **Could** you tell me the time? B: Sorry, I haven't got a watch.*

  *A: **Would you mind** repeating that question? B: **Not at all**. (= I don't mind and I will do it.)*

- to ask if you can do something.

  *A: **Can** I ask you a question?   B: Of course.*

  *A: **Could** I borrow your laptop?   B: Yes, of course.*

  *A: **May** I leave early today, please? B: No, I'm sorry. We're busy.*

  May and **could** are more polite than **can**.

Remember!

Most of the phrases are followed by the infinitive.
*Can I **help** you?*

But **would you mind** is followed by -**ing.**
*Would you mind **closing** the window?*

Talking about what is happening now

Verbs for talking about what is happening at the time of speaking (see page 69)

You use the **present continuous**:

for talking about what is happening now.

I'm playing the piano now.

Sue's shopping.

for talking about temporary situations around now.

We're staying in London at the moment.

I'm studying medicine at university.

> **Remember!**
>
> You usually use the contracted form of the verb **be** and the verb with **-ing**.
>
> *I'm staying. You're leaving. He isn't working. They aren't speaking.*

Verbs that are not used in the continuous

There are a few kinds of verb that you do not usually use in continuous forms. These are verbs related to:

- thoughts, e.g. **think**, **believe**, **know** and **understand**.

  *A: What do you **think** of the new James Bond film?*
  B: It's fantastic.

  *I don't **believe** you. It can't be true.*

  *I didn't **understand**. Can you explain it again?*

- likes and dislikes, e.g. **like**, **hate**, **prefer**.

  *I really **like** watching tennis on TV.*

  *I **prefer** hot drinks to cold drinks.*

- possessions, e.g. **have**, **own**, **belong to**.

  *I have a ring that **belonged to** my grandmother.*

  *She doesn't **have** much money.*

- senses, e.g. **feel**, **smell**, **taste** and **sound**.

  *This chicken soup **tastes** good.*

  *Have you heard their new CD? It **sounds** really good.*

  Some of these verbs do have continuous forms when they have a different meaning.

- verbs describing senses.

  *She's **smelling** the flowers.*

  *He's **tasting** the soup.*

- **have** and **think**.

have	= to possess	*He **has** two showers in his house.*
	other meanings	*A: Where's Anthony?* *B: He's **having** a shower.*
		*I'm **having** a bad day. My computer's broken and my car won't start*

think	= to believe / have an opinion	*I **think** my car is faster than yours.*
	other meanings	*I'm **thinking** of buying a new car.*
		*She **was thinking** about her last holiday.*

Giving information about activities and jobs

Talking about duties and responsibilities
(see pages 77 and 79)

Must and *have to*

When you want to say it is necessary to do something, you use **must** or **have to**.

*You **must** give your work in before the deadline.*

*We **have to** deal with customer complaints.*

*He **has to** travel to find work.*

There is sometimes a difference between **must** and **have to**. When you are stating your own opinion, you normally use **must**.

*He **must** stop working so hard.*

When you are saying what someone else considers to be necessary or when you want to show that something is not your choice, you normally use **have to**.

*I **have to** practise every day.*

*She **has to** go now.*

Mustn't and *don't have to*

You use **must not** or **mustn't** to say that it is important that something is not done or does not happen.

*You **must not** touch those switches!*

*They **mustn't** find out that I came here. Keep it secret.*

If you **do not have to** do something, it is not necessary for you to do it, but you can do it if you want.

*I **don't have to** finish my homework tonight. The teacher doesn't want it until Tuesday.*

You only use **must** for obligation and necessity in the present and the future. When you want to talk about the past, you use **had to** rather than **must**.

*I **had to** catch the six o'clock train to get to work on time.*

*Jim **had to** wear a suit.*

Need to and *needn't*

You can also use **need to** to talk about duties and responsibilities.

*You **need to** talk to your boss if you can't finish on time.*

You use **needn't** and **don't need to** in a similar way to **don't have to:** to say that it is not necessary to do something.

*You **don't need to** learn any new computing skills for the job.*

*You **don't need to** buy anything.*

*I can ask Sue to do that work. You **needn't** bother.*

You also use **needn't** when you are giving someone permission not to do something.

*You **needn't** stay any longer tonight.*

*We **needn't** go to the party if you don't want to.*

Using prepositions after certain verbs

Some common verbs are followed by one or more prepositions. Other common verbs have no preposition after them.

The table below shows you which prepositions are used with which verbs, or if prepositions are needed at all.

Verb	Preposition(s)	Verb	Preposition(s)
agree	with/to	get/be married	to
arrive	at/in	marry	
ask	–	shout	at
borrow		smile	at
get/be engaged	to	speak	to/about
hear	–	talk	to/about
laugh	at	tell	–
lend	to	think	about/of
listen	to	watch	
look	at	write	about/to

Some verbs have a direct object and no preposition.

discuss and **agree**

*I **discussed the holiday** with my parents.*

*He **agreed with** everything I said.*

speak and **tell**

*I **spoke to him** about the job.*

*I **told him** about my plans.*

Some verbs can be followed by different prepositions that can change the meaning of the sentence:

- **work for** a company or person

  *I **work for** a large multi-national company.*

- **work in** a place

  *We **work in** a very small office.*

- **work with** a person

  *I **work with** several other people who have the same qualifications.*

Modal verbs for ability (see page 130)

Talking about now

You use **can** and **can't** in the present:

- to say someone knows how to do something (or not).

  *Mel **can** drive.*

  *She **can't** speak Spanish.*

- to say someone has the ability to do something (or not).

  *He **can't** do the work. It's difficult.*

  *I **can** eat fish.*

  *I **can't** eat meat.*

- with verbs like **see**, **hear**, **watch**, **feel**, **remember**, **smell**, **touch**.

  *I **can't remember** your name.*

  *She **can see** the film tomorrow.*

Talking about the past

You use **could** and **couldn't** in the past.

*I **couldn't** go shopping yesterday. The shops were closed.*

*She **could** read when she was 5 years old.*

Talking about past events and situations

Verbs for talking about the past (see page 27)

You use the **past simple** for events that happened in the past. The past simple of a regular verb is formed by adding **-ed** to the base form of the regular verb.

*My son **opened** his present and **smiled** at me.*

*I **climbed** over the fence as fast as I could.*

If you are talking about the general past, or about regular or habitual actions in the past, you also use the past simple.

*She **lived** just outside London.*

*We often **saw** his dog sitting outside his house.*

Remember!

There are also many verbs with irregular forms.

be – was/were

become – became

get – got

give – gave

go – went

have – had

say – said

see – saw

teach – taught

wake – woke

wear – wore

write – wrote

Talking about past situations and habits

You can talk about past situations and habits by using the form **used to** and then the verb in the base form.

*I **used to be** overweight, but now I eat healthy food to stay slim.*

Read the following dialogue. Two people have just met in the street.

A: *Excuse me. I think I know you. I'm sure I recognize you.*

B: *Oh yes! Me too! **Did you use to study** at Liverpool University in the 1990s?*

A: *Yes, I did! Oh, your name is Daisy, isn't it? You **used to live** next door to me, if I remember correctly. I'm Anne-Marie.*

B: *Of course, yes, Anne-Marie. I remember now. **Didn't you use to study** music? How's that going?*

A: *Oh, I'm afraid I don't play the guitar any more. I work in a bank now. And how about you?*

B: *Well that's strange, because I actually **used to work** in a bank but I've just left because I want to become a firefighter!*

Remember!

Used to is a past form. There is no present form. You use **used** in statements, but in the negative and in questions you use **use**.

*James **used to have** long hair but now he's bald.*

*He **didn't use to be** friendly.*

*Where **did you use to live?***

Talking about things in progress in the past

Past continuous

You use the past continuous to describe continuous actions in progress at a particular time in the past.

*When the clock struck midnight, Anna **was laughing** at something on her phone. Her sister, Helen, **was sleeping** in a chair and Helen's two children **were watching** a film on TV.*

You can use the past continuous with the past simple to compare two actions. You use the past continuous when you describe the longer action.

*What **was happening** when you took the photo?*

*I **was sitting** on the beach when I saw the boat.*

Time clauses and adverbs: before, after, then, when, while, as

You use **before** and **after** with a verb to show when things happen.

*He did his homework **before** he had dinner.*

*He did his homework **after** he had dinner.*

You use **during** before a noun or noun phrase to mean **'throughout that period of time'**.

*Prices increased **during the winter.***

*We practised speaking in pairs several times **during the lesson.***

You use **when** to show that one thing happens right after another.

*She opened her presents **when** she woke up.*

*He turned on his computer **when** he got home.*

You use **while** to show that one thing happens at the same time as another thing.

*He usually does his homework **while** he watches TV.*

*She borrowed my car **while** I was on holiday.*

You can also begin a sentence with **when**, **while**, **before**, **after**.

__When__ he got home, he turned on his computer.

__While__ I was on holiday, she borrowed my car.

When you use the past continuous, you can compare two actions using **when**, **while** and **as**.

I was swimming in the sea __when__ it started raining.

I texted my friend __while__ I was waiting for the bus.

__As__ we were leaving home, the phone rang.

You can put the two parts of these sentences in a different order.

__When__ it started raining I was swimming in the sea.

Remember!

You use **when** before the past simple and **while** or **as** before the past continuous

Connecting ideas (see page 35)

Basic linking words

We use some basic linking words to connect parts of a sentence.

And adds two things together.

She used to play basketball __and__ football.

I had a shower __and__ ate my dinner.

But makes a contrast.

I watched the first film __but__ I didn't watch the second one

= I watched the first film __but not__ the second one.

Or links two negative things.

I don't like fruit __or__ vegetables.

Ben didn't eat the pizza __or__ the rice.

Because shows a reason.

We couldn't improve the service __because__ we didn't have enough money.

I don't want to go running __because__ it's dark.

Remember!

You don't need to repeat the subject after **and** and **or**.

I love reading __and__ drawing. (I love reading and I love drawing.)

I don't like Pedro __or__ Sally. (I don't like Pedro or I don't like Sally.)

Adding ideas

As well as **and**, we use **also**, **in addition**, **furthermore** and **similarly** to link similar ideas together.

Also can be used at the start of a sentence or between two clauses.

Social networking sites help us to find information and __also__ make new friends.

__Also__, these sites help us reconnect with old friends.

In addition, **furthermore** and **similarly** are usually used at the start of a new sentence.

I hope to go to the museum when I'm in Madrid. __In addition__, I'd like to see the art gallery.

I was not happy with the food. __Furthermore__, the waiters were rude.

You can't use your phone in the classroom. __Similarly__, you have to switch it off in the hall.

Contrasting ideas

As well as **but**, we use **although**, **even though**, **however**, **nevertheless**, **nonetheless**, **on the other hand** to contrast two different ideas.

Although and **even though** can be used at the start of a sentence or between two clauses.

__Although__ she was ill, she worked hard.

She worked hard __although__ she was ill.

__Even though__ they left at ten, they arrived on time.

They arrived on time __even though__ they didn't leave until ten.

However, **nevertheless**, **nonetheless** and **on the other hand** are usually used at the start of a new sentence.

They started the work several months ago. __However__, they haven't finished it yet.

They buy most of their food in the supermarket. __Nevertheless__, they go to the market to buy speciality foods.

There was an increase in sales in December. __Nonetheless__, there was an overall decrease.

England has better language schools. __On the other hand__, it has worse weather.

(See *Talking about cause and effect* for linking words connected with results: *so, therefore, consequently, as a result.*)

Describing places and things

Using *there* and *it*

You use **There is/There are** to say something exists.

> **There is** a school in my village.

> **There are** three shops on my street.

You can use the contraction **There's** but not ~~There're~~.

> **There weren't** any tall buildings until the 20th century.

> **There have been** a lot of tourists this summer.

> **There will be** more accommodation next year.

> **There will be** a new transport system.

You use it/they to talk about something that was mentioned before.

> **There are** some very old houses in my town. **They're** made of stone.

> **There's** a park in the middle of my street. **It's got** a new playground.

You use **it** before **be**:

- to talk about the weather.
  > **It's** very cold in the winter.
- to talk about time.
  > **It was** very late when they arrived.
- to express your opinions.
  > **It was** a really beautiful place.
  > **It's going to be** a very expensive trip.

You can also use **it** with **take**.

> A: How long **does it take** to get there?
> B: About three hours.

Articles

You use **the** when:

- it is clear which person or thing you are talking about.
  > **The street**'s very empty.
  > **The volunteers** meet on Sundays.
- there is only one of these people or things.
  > I saw **the President** on TV yesterday.
  > **The moon** is very bright tonight.

You use **a/an** when:

- you have not talked about something before.
  > I saw **a good film** yesterday.
  > We live in **an apartment**.
- you say what jobs people do.
  > My brother's **a famous footballer**.
  > I'm training to be **a doctor**.

Sometimes there is no article before a noun.

She's ...	She's going ...
at work	to work
at home	home
at school, university	to school, university
in bed	to bed
in hospital	to hospital
in prison	to prison
in church	to church

Proper nouns

Proper nouns are nouns that refer to particular named people, places or things. They are always spelt with a capital letter.

> We spent a day in **New York** and saw the **Statue of Liberty**.

> I saw **Jenny** on **Saturday**.

> He was born in **Poland** but later moved to **France**.

Some proper nouns are used with **the** and others are not. We call this the zero article.

You use **the** with:

- deserts, oceans and rivers.
  > the Gobi Desert, the Nile, the Atlantic (Ocean)
- named buildings or attractions.
  > the Pyramids, the Eiffel Tower, the Taj Mahal, the Tate Gallery

You use zero article with:

- cities and streets.
  > San Francisco, Park Street, Seventh Avenue
- mountains and lakes.
  > Lake Superior, Mount Everest
- continents.
  > Africa, Australia

Countries

You do not use **the** with the names of most countries. There are some where you do, however, and you need to remember these. Notice that you use **the** with countries that are states, kingdoms and republics or with plural nouns.

> Canada, Indonesia, France, Russia, Germany

> the USA, the UK, the Maldives, the Netherlands, the Czech Republic

Comparing things

Comparatives and superlatives (see page 25)

Comparatives

You use **than** to compare two things.

> The rent was **higher** in 2014 **than** it was in 2013.
>
> The cottage is **prettier than** the house.

For longer adjectives, you say **more** before the adjective.

> The city is **more expensive** than the country.

Superlatives

You use **the** + adjective + **-est** to say which one is the most.

> **The highest** rents were in the North.
>
> It's **the prettiest** house in the street.

For longer adjectives, you say **the most** before the adjective.

> History is **the most interesting** subject.

Adjective	Comparative	Superlative
slow	slower	the slowest
hot	hotter	the hottest
safe	safer	the safest
dirty	dirtier	the dirtiest

Irregular short adjectives

Some adjectives are different from the examples above.

Adjective	Comparative	Superlative
bad	worse	the worst
good	better	the best
far	further	the furthest

> #### Remember!
>
> **Spelling**
>
> If a short adjective ends with a vowel and a consonant, you double the consonant.
>
> big → bigger → the biggest
>
> If an adjective ends in **-y**, you change it to **-i**.
>
> happy → happier → the happiest

less than, the least

You can also make comparisons using:

- **less ... than** ...

  You can use **less ... than ...** with most longer adjectives.

  > Reading books is **less interesting than** playing computer games. (Playing computer games is more interesting than reading books.)

- **the least** ...

  > Why don't you buy these shoes? They're **the least expensive**. (They're the cheapest.)

(not) as ... as

You use **as ... as ...** to compare people or things that are similar in some way.

> London is **as dirty as** New York.
>
> The airport was **as crowded as** ever.
>
> I am **as good as** she is.

You can make a negative comparison using **not as ... as ...** or **not so ... as ....**

> The rooms are **not as comfortable as** they appear to be.
>
> The food was**n't** quite **as good as** yesterday.
>
> The palace is **not so old as** I thought.

Modifying adverbs used with comparisons (see pages 31 and 47)

We often use other words with comparisons to emphasize or limit any similarity.

> Your picture is (not) **exactly** the same as mine.
>
> Your picture is **extremely** similar to mine.
>
> Your picture is **quite** different from mine.
>
> Your picture is **a bit /a little** like mine.

Linking words that show similarities and differences (see page 31)

We also use words like **as well as** and **too** to show that things are similar.

> Rice is popular in India **as well as** in China.
>
> Rice is popular in India and in China, **too**.

We use words like **but**, **except (for)** and **apart from** to show that things are different.

> Most houses in the UK are made of brick, **but** blocks of flats are made of concrete.
>
> The building was clean, **except** the bathroom, which was very dirty.
>
> Many homes in the UK are made of brick, **apart from** blocks of flats, which are made of concrete.

Describing pictures, graphs and charts

Verbs for describing pictures and graphs

When you talk about a picture or graph, you can use the verbs **show**, **illustrate** and **compare** in the present simple to introduce your description.

> This picture **shows** two people.
>
> The diagram **illustrates** the stages of the process.
>
> The graph **compares** two things.

Nouns for describing quantities in graphs and charts (see page 48)

Percentage, **amount**, **number**, **proportion** and **quantity** can all be used to describe the quantities shown in graphs and charts.

> Teenagers spend a smaller **amount** on buying DVDs than older people.
>
> The **percentage** of people who watched horror films decreased.
>
> The **number** of people who prefer comedies is very small.
>
> The **proportion** of people who watched action films increased.

Verbs and nouns for describing trends

When you describe trends and movements in a graph or chart, you can use can use **increase**, **decrease**, **rise**, **fall**, **drop** as nouns or verbs.

> There has been **an increase** in interest in wave power.
>
> Interest in wave power has **increased**.
>
> There was **a rise** in unemployment.
>
> Unemployment **rose** last year.
>
> There is likely to be **a fall** in prices.
>
> Prices are likely **to fall**.
>
> We can see **a drop** in temperature.
>
> We can see that the temperature is **dropping**.

Adjectives and adverbs for describing trends

It is common to use adjectives and adverbs like **gradual/gradually**, **steady/steadily**, **sharp/sharply** and **rapid/rapidly** to give more information about trends in graphs and charts.

adjective + noun

> There was **a gradual decrease** last year.
>
> There has been **a steady rise** over the past two months.
>
> The graph shows **a rapid increase** in 2014.
>
> We can see **a sharp fall** in January.

verb + adverb

> These figures **have decreased gradually**.
>
> The temperature **is rising steadily**.
>
> Numbers **increased rapidly** last year.
>
> Imports **fell sharply** in 2013.

Describing quantities

Much, many, a lot (of), a little, a few (see page 25)

How much and How many

- You use **How much** in questions with uncountable nouns.

  > **How much** time do most teenagers spend on their homework?
  >
  > **How much** studying did you do at school?

- You use **How many** in questions with countable nouns.

  > **How many** people have smart phones?
  >
  > **How many** hours do you spend travelling?

Talking about quantity

To talk about a small quantity, you can use **a little**, **a few**, **not much** and **not many.**

To talk about a large quantity, you can use **a lot of** and **lots of**.

For countable nouns you use **lots of**, **a lot of**, **a few** and **not many**.

> There are **lots of** students.
>
> There are **a lot of** teenagers.
>
> There are **a few** older students.
>
> There are **not many** younger boys.

For uncountable nouns you use **lots of**, **a lot of**, **a little** and **not much**.

> There is **not much** help.
>
> There is **a lot of** money.

Remember!

A little is more positive than **not much**, and **a few** is more positive than **not many**.

> There are **a few** shops in the village. (= There are five or six shops. I think this is enough.)
>
> There are**n't many** shops in the village. (= There are five or six shops. I don't think this is enough.)
>
> There is **a little** information on their website. (= I think this is enough.)
>
> There is**n't much** information on their website. (= I don't think this is enough.)

Few / A few and little / a little

These sentences show the difference between **few**, **a few**, **little** and **a little**.

> I have **few** friends. = I don't have many friends.
>
> I have **a few** DVDs. = I have some DVDs.
>
> There was **very little** food left at the end of the party. = There wasn't much food left.
>
> There was **a little** food left at the end of the party. = There was some food left.

A few (of), some (of), most (of), all (of)

You can use **a few**, **some**, **most** and **all (of)** + noun to describe sections or parts of a group of people or things.

> **Most children** go to school.
>
> **A few of us** have been to the cinema this week.
>
> **Some people in the group** reported that they had changed their diet.
>
> **Some of the work** is difficult.
>
> **All of the girls** could swim, but only **a few of them** could dive.

> **Remember!**
>
> **A few** is only used with countable nouns. Use **less** to describe uncountable quantities.
>
> **Less** time is spent doing homework in the summer.

Adverbs for talking about approximate numbers

Sometimes, you need to talk about numbers in a less precise way. You can use adverbs like **approximately**, **just over**, **just under**, **almost**, **nearly**, **around** and **about** in front of a number or quantity if you are not sure of the exact number.

> The number rose by **approximately** 20 per cent in 2015.
>
> **Just over** a third of visitors were aged 30–40.
>
> **Just under** a quarter of cinema visitors are between 15 and 25 years old.
>
> **Almost** half of the children had been to the cinema in the holidays.
>
> There was an improvement in **nearly** all the teams.
>
> **Around** two hundred protestors were arrested.
>
> I saw **about** nine dogs on the beach.

Several and a couple (of)

You can only use **several** and **a couple of** before countable nouns.

> There are **a couple of** people waiting for you.
>
> I've been to **several** football matches this year.

Talking about events that began in the past

Present perfect (see pages 40 and 71)

Uses of the present perfect

You use the present perfect when you want to talk about the present effects of something that happened or started in the past.

You can use the present perfect:

- to talk about something that happened in the past but that is still important in the present.

  > What's the matter, Ann? **I've lost** my purse.

- to describe something that started in the past and is still happening now.

  > A: Do you know this part of town?
  >
  > B: Yes, **I've lived** here for ten years.

- to talk about things you have done at some time in the past.

  > **I've been** to America three times.
  >
  > **I've** never **read** any Harry Potter books.

- with **just** to talk about the recent past.

  > **I've just finished** my exams. I'm so happy.
  >
  > A: Do you want some of my chocolate?
  >
  > B: No thanks, **I've just eaten**.

- with **ever** to ask questions to find out things that people have done.

  > A: **Have** you **ever eaten** Japanese food?
  >
  > B: Yes, many times.

- with **yet** and **already**.

  > **Have** you **done** your homework **yet**?
  >
  > Don't tell me what happens at the end of the film. I **haven't seen** it **yet**.
  >
  > They don't need to raise the price of petrol. It**'s already increased**.

> **Remember!**
>
> You use **already** in positive sentences and **yet** in negative sentences and questions.

Form of the present perfect

have/has + past participle

The past participle of regular verbs is formed by adding **-ed** to the infinitive. If the infinitive ends in **-e**, you add only **-d**.

Infinitive	Past participle
work	worked
change	changed
finish	finished

*Most of the staff **have worked** there for a short time.*

*She's **changed** her behaviour since she met her boyfriend.*

*I **haven't finished** it yet.*

Remember!

You can use a short form of **have**.

I've = I have

they haven't = they have not

he's = he has

she hasn't = she has not

we've = we have

Many common verbs have irregular forms. Here are a few.

Infinitive	Past participle
be	been
have	had
go	gone
see	seen
eat	eaten

Present perfect with *been* and *gone*

*Sam's **gone** to the shops to buy a newspaper. He'll be back in a few minutes. (= Sam is still at the shops.)*

*Julia's **been** to the shops so we've got enough food for dinner. (= Julia has gone to the shops and come back.)*

For and *since*

We often use the present perfect:

• with **for** (for a period of time).

*He's worked there **for** three months.*

• with **since** (from a point in time).

*I've lived in Paris **since** 2010.*

3 months **2010 NOW**   **July NOW (October)**

started work   moved to Paris
still working there   still living in Paris

Talking about plans and arrangements

Talking about future intentions

When you are talking about plans you have already made or what someone else has decided to do, you use **going to**.

*I'**m going to** learn a new sport.*

*They'**re going to** graduate next year.*

*She'**s going to** be an actress.*

Remember!

You do not normally use **going to** with the verb **go**. You usually just say **I'm going** rather than **I'm going to go**.

*A: What **are** you **going to** do next year?*

*B: I'**m going** back to university.*

When you are announcing a decision you have just made or are about to make, you use **will**.

*I'm tired. I think I'**ll** go to bed.*

*I'**ll** ring you tonight.*

Talking about future arrangements
(see pages 8 and 91)

When you talk about firm plans or arrangements for the future, you often use the present continuous.

*What **are** you **doing** this weekend?*

*I'**m getting** the train to London this afternoon.*

*We'**re going** to that new restaurant tonight.*

When you talk about something that will happen at a definite time in the future or as part of a schedule, you often use the present simple. You often use a time expression too.

*The train **leaves** in a few minutes.*

*My holiday **starts** on Monday.*

*When **do** your exams **finish**?*

When you promise or offer to do something in the future, you use **will**.

*I'**ll text** you when I get there.*

*I'**ll give** it back to you next week.*

You can also use **will** when you are sure about something in the future.

*She's working late tonight. She'**ll be** home after 7.00.*

*We **won't be** at school tomorrow. It's a holiday.*

- **positive**

You can use either **will** or **'ll**. These forms do not change.

> *I'll / I will see you next week.*
>
> *They'll be here at 6 p.m.*

- **negative**

You can use either **will not** or **won't**. These forms do not change.

> *She won't / will not be here until this evening.*
>
> *We won't / will not be very late.*

- **question**

> *Will you call me when you get there?*
>
> *Will we be home by tomorrow?*

Talking about plans you aren't sure about

May and might

You use **may** and **might** to talk about future plans that are possible, but you are not sure about.

> A: *Have you got any plans for this evening?*
>
> B: *I might go to the cinema or I may just stay at home and watch a DVD.*

The meaning of **may** and **might** in these sentences is the same.

Will probably

You use **will probably** when you are more sure about something.

> *I've missed the last bus. I could get a taxi but I'll probably walk home.*

Could

You can also use **could** to talk about something that is possible in the present or future.

Describing a sequence or process (see page 63)

The passive voice

The passive is often used for describing processes, usually in the present tense.

> *The seeds are mixed with salt.*
>
> *The fruit is usually picked in early September.*
>
> *The goods are now ready to be delivered.*

(see *Passive verbs in the present and past*)

Sequence adverbs (see pages 61 and 87)

We often use adverbs such as **first, first of all, firstly; second, secondly; third, thirdly; lastly, finally** to order the main points of a talk, essay or set of instructions. These words act as signposts when a new idea is mentioned.

> *Firstly/First of all, you need to decide which type of product you want.*
>
> *Secondly, you should have a budget in mind.*
>
> *Thirdly, make sure you research what reviewers say about different brands.*
>
> *Finally/Lastly, think about where you want to put it.*

We also use sequencers to help clarify the sequence of a process or activity. As well as the ones above we can use **then, next, after that, some time, eventually** to focus on the time period.

> *First, the animal dies.*
>
> *Next, it is covered in mud.*
>
> *After some time, the animal is completely buried in the mud.*
>
> *Then the soil turns into rock.*
>
> *Eventually, the animal becomes a fossil.*

Describing things and their purposes

Adjective order

Most adjectives can be used in a noun phrase, after determiners and numbers if there are any, or in front of the noun.

> *She had a beautiful ring.*
>
> *She bought a loaf of white bread.*
>
> *Six new episodes of the TV show will be filmed.*

You often want to add more information to a noun than you can with one adjective.

When you use more than one adjective, one with a more general meaning such as **good**, **bad**, **nice** or **lovely** usually comes before one with a more specific meaning such as **comfortable**, **clean** or **dirty**.

> You live in a **nice big** house.
>
> It was a **naughty little** dog.
>
> She was wearing a **lovely pink** suit.
>
> I sat in a **nice comfortable** armchair in the corner.

Adjectives with a more specific meaning belong to six main types, but you are unlikely ever to use all six types in the same sentence. If you did, you would normally put them in the following order:

size → age → shape → colour → nationality → material

This means that if you want to use an 'age' adjective and a 'nationality' adjective, you put the 'age' adjective first.

> We bought some **old Chinese** vases.

Similarly, a 'shape' adjective normally comes before a 'colour' adjective.

> We found some **round black** stones.

Other combinations of adjectives follow the same order. Note that 'material' means any substance, not only cloth.

> There was a **large round wooden** table in the room.
>
> The man was carrying a **small black plastic** bag.

Linking adjectives together

When you use two adjectives of the same type, you use **and** to link them. With three or more adjectives, you link the last two with **and**, and put commas after the others.

> The day was **hot and dusty**.
>
> The house was **old, damp and smelly**.
>
> We felt **hot, tired and thirsty**.
>
> When you are linking two negative adjectives, you use **or**.
>
> My job **isn't interesting or well-paid**.
>
> We went to see a romantic comedy at the cinema.
> Unfortunately, **it wasn't funny or romantic!**

Prepositions for talking about the purpose of actions or things (see page 49)

For

You use **for** in front of a noun phrase or **-ing** form when you state the purpose of an object, action or activity.

> Some planes are **for** domestic flights; others are **for** international flights.

> The bowl was used **for** mixing flour and water.

You use **for** in front of a noun phrase when you are saying why someone does something.

> We went to the main hall **for** the lecture.

With

If you do something **with** a tool or object, you do it using that tool or object.

> Clean the floor **with** a mop.
>
> He tapped the table **with** his hand.
>
> You use **with** after verbs like **fight** or **argue**.
>
> He was always fighting **with** his brother.

Passive verbs in the present and past

The difference between passive and active

When you want to talk about the person or thing that performs an action, you use the active.

> Polluted water **kills** sea life and fish.
>
> They **stored** the furniture in a large warehouse.

When you want to focus on the person or thing that is affected by an action, you use the passive.

> Sea life and fish **are killed** by polluted water.
>
> The furniture was **stored** in a large warehouse.

You form the passive with the verb **be** and the past participle (e.g. **made**, **told**).

Passive form: *be* + past participle

Present simple passive: Paper **is made** from wood.

Past simple passive: The building **was completed** in 1853.

Present perfect passive: All the rooms **have** just **been painted.**

Question forms

> A: When **is** the room **cleaned**?
>
> B: Every day.
>
> A: When **was** the film **made**?
>
> B: In 2012.
>
> A: **Have** you **been served** yet?
>
> B: No, I'm still waiting.

You often use the passive when the object of the verb is more important than the subject, so

> They **completed** the building in 1853.

becomes

> The building **was completed** in 1853.

In passive sentences, you use **by** before the person or thing that causes the action (the agent).

> *J.K. Rowling* **wrote** *the Harry Potter books.* (active)
>
> *The Harry Potter books* **were written by** *J.K. Rowling.* (passive)

If you do not know who the agent is, or it is clear who it is, you don't need to use **by**.

> *His wallet* **was stolen** *(by someone) while he was on holiday.*
>
> *Letters* **are delivered** *(by the postman) every morning.*

Speculating and making predictions

Using *will* and *going* to to make predictions

When you make predictions about the future that are based on general beliefs, opinions or attitudes, you use **will**.

> *The weather tomorrow* **will** *be warm and sunny.*
>
> *I'm sure you'll enjoy your visit to my city.*

When you use facts or events in the present situation as evidence for a prediction, you use **be + going to**.

> *It's* **going to** *rain. (I can see black clouds.)*
>
> *I'm* **going to** *be late for the meeting. (I woke up too late.)*

Talking about possibility (see pages 13 and 56)

When you are not completely sure about something, you can use the modal verbs **must**, **might**, **may** or **could**.

Must

When you are fairly sure that something is true, you use **must**.

> *This* **must** *be a new film; I haven't seen it before.*

Can't

When you are fairly sure that something is not true, you use **can't** or **cannot**.

> *It* **can't** *be the right size; it's too small.*

Could, may and might

When you are not sure whether something is true or not, you use **could**, **may** or **might**.

The ban on smoking **might** upset people.

> *The new strategy* **might** *not work.*
>
> *The new drugs* **could** *help to improve people's health.*
>
> *The police* **may** *not be able to find the thief.*

must be	sure that something is true
can't be	sure that something is not true
could be/might be	not sure that something is true

Talking about cause and effect (see page 103)

Linking words to describe causes and effects

You can use **so**, **therefore**, **as a result**, **consequently**, to link causes and effects.

cause → effect

> *There are more doctors* **so** *people are living longer.*
>
> *There are more doctors and people are living longer* **as a result.**

Therefore, **as a result**, **consequently** are used to connect sentences.

> *Exercise keeps people healthy.* **Therefore**, *people who exercise regularly live longer.*
>
> *It poured with rain.* **As a result**, *the game was cancelled.*
>
> *I didn't study hard enough.* **Consequently**, *I failed my exam.*

You can use **because**, **as**, **since**, **as a result of**, **due to** to link effects to causes.

effect → cause

> *People are living longer* **because** *there are more doctors.*
>
> *People are living longer* **as** *there are more doctors.*
>
> *People are living longer* **since** *there are more doctors.*
>
> *People are living longer* **due to** *an increase in doctors.*
>
> *People are living longer* **as a result of** *more doctors.*

> ### Remember!
>
> Notice that **as a result of** and **due to** are followed by a noun phrase.

Zero conditional for facts

You use the zero conditional when you talk about something that is always true.

If + present simple + present simple

If *you* **heat** *water,* *it* **boils**.

present simple + **if** + present simple

You **get** *fat* **if** *you* **eat** *too much chocolate.*

First conditional for possibility

You use the first conditional to talk about things that can happen in the future.

If	Present simple	Will
If	*you* **take** *a map,*	*you* **won't** *get lost.*
If	*you* **work** *hard,*	*you'll pass your exams.*
If	*the weather* **is** *fine*	*I'll walk.*

You can also put the part of the sentence with **if** second.

*You won't get lost **if** you take a map.*

> **Remember!**
>
> Notice that after **if** you use the present simple, not **will**.
>
> *If you **remember** this, you'**ll do** well!*
>
> ~~If you'll remember this, you'll do well!~~

Sometimes, we use the imperative or other modal verbs instead of **will**.

> *If you aren't sure what to do, **ask** your teacher.*
> *If people exercise every day, they **may** live longer.*
> *If it rains, I **might** not go.*

Second conditional for unlikely situations

The second conditional is used to talk about things that are unlikely to happen or things that are hypothetical.

> *If I had the money, I would buy a car.*
> *What would you do if you won a million dollars?*

There are two parts to the second conditional: one part contains the **past simple** (If I **had** the money) and the second part contains **would** (I **would** buy a car).

if	+	past simple	+	would
If	all illnesses **were** cured,	everybody **would** be happy.		
If	he **worked** harder,	he'**d** pass his exams.		
If	there **were** no police,	there **would** be more crime.		

> **Remember!**
>
> You do not normally use **would** in both parts of the sentence.
>
> ~~If all illnesses would be cured, everybody would be happy.~~
>
> *If all illnesses were cured, everybody **would** be happy.*

You can also use **could** or **might** instead of **would** if you are not certain about the result.

> *If people stopped smoking, they **could** save money.*
> *If children had more exercise, they **might** be fitter.*

Asking for and giving advice

Should and ought to (see pages 99 and 110)

You use **should** and **ought to** when you give advice or ask for advice.

> *People in Europe **should** eat less junk food.*
> *You **shouldn't** work so hard. You **ought to** relax a bit more.*
> *I've lost my passport. What **should** I do?*

Had ('d) better

You can also use **had better** for giving advice.

> *You'**d better** get more petrol. It's very low.*

> **Remember!**
>
> In negative sentences you say **had ('d) better not**.
>
> *We're having a big meal later so **you'd better not** eat too much now.*

Talking about feelings

-ing and -ed adjectives

Many adjectives are formed from verbs by adding **-ing** or **-ed**.

Many **-ing** adjectives describe the effect that something has on your feelings, or on the feelings of people in general.

> *Last year, there was a **surprising** number of accidents.* (= The number surprises you.)

Many **-ed** adjectives describe people's feelings. They have a passive meaning.

> *She was genuinely **surprised** at what happened to her pet* (= She feels surprise because of what happened.)

amazing	amazed
boring	bored
exciting	excited
surprising	surprised
terrifying	terrified
tiring	tired
worrying	worried
frightening	frightened
interesting	interested
shocking	shocked
embarrassing	embarrassed
disappointing	disappointed
confusing	confused
annoying	annoyed
pleasing	pleased

Like other adjectives, **-ing** and **-ed** adjectives can be:

- used in front of a noun.

    This is a **shocking** news report.

    I think it's the most **terrifying** story ever written.

    The **worried** police cancelled the football match.

- used after linking verbs.

    It's **amazing** what volunteers can do.

    The present situation is **terrifying**.

    I am not **satisfied** with the work they have done.

    Everyone was **worried**.

- modified by adverbials such as **a bit**, **quite**, **really**, **very**, **extremely**.

    The film was **quite boring**.

    There is nothing **very surprising** in this.

    She was **quite embarrassed** at his behaviour.

A small number of **-ed** adjectives are mainly used after linking verbs such as **be**, **become** or **feel**.

    The Brazilians are **pleased** with the results.

Expressing ideas and opinions (see page 34)

Phrases to introduce opinions

There are several different phrases you can use to introduce your opinion.

    I believe taking photos is a good way to record important events.

    I don't think videos are as useful.

    In my opinion, photos are more important.

    I agree that it isn't possible to buy happiness.

You can also use a range of phrases to refer to other people's opinion. Note that we don't have to use the noun **people**.

    Many (people) argue that big events are more memorable than small ones.

    Some (people) claim that the Internet makes people lazy.

    Many believe that the arts are more important than sport. **Others say** that sport is more exciting.

Using -ing forms as nouns

When you want to talk about an action, activity or process in a general way, you can use a noun that has the same form as the **-ing** participle of a verb.

They can be the subject or object of a clause.

    Swimming is a great sport.

    The **closing** of so many factories left thousands of people unemployed.

    Some people have never done any **public speaking**.

    As a child, his interests were **drawing** and **stamp collecting.**

Noun phrases with **-ing** forms are often used when asking for or giving opinions about general topics.

    Do you agree that **learning to play an instrument** is a good idea?

    They don't agree that **watching too much TV** makes children lazy.

    I think **listening to music** helps you relax.

Adverbs that introduce further explanation (see page 28)

You use some adverbs to give more information or to say what you think about a sentence or part of a sentence.

actually, in fact
People think music lessons are expensive, but **actually**, you don't need much money to enjoy music.

basically
I found Lost Island 2 really boring. It was **basically** too similar to Lost Island 1.

fortunately, unfortunately
I was worried that the task would be too difficult for me but **fortunately**, was able to do it.

I'm very busy at the moment. **Unfortunately**, I'll have to cancel our meeting.

luckily, unluckily
The weather was terrible. **Luckily**, we didn't need to go out.

moreover
The article is badly written. **Moreover**, it is not always accurate.

despite
Crime is increasing **despite** the efforts of the police.

unsurprisingly
Unsurprisingly, not everyone agrees that the situation is improving.

Using phrases to give yourself time to think (see page 78)

When you speak or answer a question, you can use a filler word or phrase like **um**, **uh**, **er**, **you know**, to avoid

…esitation. Fillers help you speak naturally and fluently when you give longer answers.

I think this tradition is important. **I mean**, it's a serious thing but it's fun.

I guess it's hard to change the way you do things.

Let me see, I'd like to work in the hospitality industry.

That's interesting. I hadn't thought about that question before …

I suppose it depends on how old you are.

I'm not sure, but I think I'd prefer to go to university abroad.

William Collins' dream of knowledge for all began with the publication of his first book in 1819.

A self-educated mill worker, he not only enriched millions of lives, but also founded a flourishing publishing house. Today, staying true to this spirit, Collins books are packed with inspiration, innovation and practical expertise. They place you at the centre of a world of possibility and give you exactly what you need to explore it.

Collins. Freedom to teach.

HarperCollins*Publishers*
The News Building,
1 London Bridge Street
London SE1 9GF

First edition 2016

Reprint 10 9 8 7 6 5 4 3 2 1

© HarperCollins*Publishers* 2016

ISBN 978-0-00-813917-9

Collins® is a registered trademark of HarperCollins*Publishers* Ltd.

www.collinselt.com

A catalogue record for this book is available from the British Library

Authors: Fiona Aish
Jane Short
Rhona Snelling
Jo Tomlinson
Els Van Geyte
Publisher: Celia Wigley
Commissioning editor: Lisa Todd
Editors: Michael Appleton, Helen Marsden
Cover design: Angela English
Typeset in India by Jouve
Printed in Italy by Grafica Veneta S.p.A

Photograph Acknowledgments:
All photos are from Shutterstock

p6: **Tom Wang**; p8: **YanLev**; p8: **Rahhal**; p10: **ZouZou**; p13: **Monkey Business Images**; p16: **Dmitrijs Dmitrijevs**; p19: **BRG. photography**; p21: **Ilike**; p21: **Shannon Heryet**; p21: **Rido**; p21: **Olga Danylenko**; p22: **Air Images**; p26: **sunsinger**; p28: **Golden Pixels LLC**; p30: **Becky Wass**; p32: **Kamira Editorial**; p32: **qingqing**; p36: **Bryan Pollard**; p38: **wavebreakmedia**; p38: **Dariush M**; p39: **IR Stone**; p46: **Gilmanshin**; p48: **REDAV**; p50: **Yomka**; p51: **Ruth Black**; p52: **Stefano Tintil**; p53: **DmitriMaruta**; p54: **picture5479**; p56: **Repina Valeriya**; p58: **Denis Burdin**; p60: **ermess**; p60: **Onuma Yeerong**; p66: **wk1003mike**; p69: **enciktat**; p74: **wavebreakmedia**; p74: **KPG_Jsco**; p74: **gresei**; p74: **Andrey_Popov**; p74: **Vincent St. Thomas**; p74: **Sergii Korolko**; p76: **Snvv**; p77: **Goodluz**; p77: **Asier Romero**; p78: **William Perugini**; p79: **Pressmaster**; p86: **Galyna Andrushko**; p87: **Pagina**; p89: **Marish**; p89: **Lars Zahner**; p96: **Stokkete**; p96: **Africa Studio**; p96: **Robyn Mackenzie**; p96: **ffolas**; p96: **Richard Semik**; p96: **Sean Nel**; p96: **R.legosyn**; p96: **TAGSTOCK1**; p104: **Ronald Sumners**; p104: **Pressmaster**; p105: **TonyV3112**; p106: **Yauhen_D**; p109: **Gajus**; p111: **B Studio**; p116: **Zadorozhnyi Viktor**; p118: **hin225**; p121: **Monkey Business Images**; p122: **Rueangrit Srisuk**